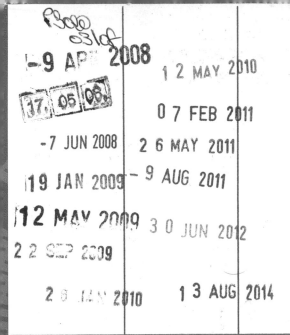

PETERBOROUGH

CITY COUNCIL

24 HOUR RENEWAL LINE 08458 505606

This book is to be returned on or before the latest date shown above, but may be renewed up to three times, if the book is not in demand. Ask at your local library for details.

Please note that charges are made on books returned late.

D1386548

Written by Pat Le...
Updated by Nicol...

Published by Thor... ...s Cook Publishing
A division of Thon... ...k Tour Operations ...
Company registra... ...on No ...1450464 England
The Thomas Cook ... ...Road
Peterborough PE3 ...
Email: sales@thor...
www.thomascook... ...blisl...

Produced by The C... ...ntent Works Ltd
Aston Court, Kings... ...ead Business Park, Frederick Pla...
High Wycombe, Bu... ...cks HP11 8LA
www.thecontentworks.com

Series design based on an original concept by Studio 183 Limited

ISBN: 978-1-84157-957-3

First edition © 2006 Thomas Cook Publishing
This second edition © 2008 Thomas Cook Publishing
Text © Thomas Cook Publishing
Maps © Thomas Cook Publishing/PCGraphics (UK) Limited
Transport map © Communicarta Limited

Series Editor: Kelly Anne Pipes
Production/DTP: Steven Collins

Printed and bound in Spain by GraphyCems

Cover photography (Nyhavn) © Trond Hillestad/Photolibrary

CONTENTS

SYMBOLS KEY

The following symbols are used throughout this book:

ⓐ address ☏ telephone ⓦ website address ⓔ email
🕐 opening times Ⓝ public transport connections ❶ important

The following symbols are used on the maps:

𝒊	information office	▪	points of interest
✈	airport	O	city
✚	hospital	O	large town
🛡	police station	○	small town
🚍	bus station	═	motorway
🚉	railway station	—	main road
Ⓜ	metro	—	minor road
✝	cathedral	—	railway
❶	numbers denote featured cafés & restaurants		

Hotels and restaurants are graded by approximate price as follows:
£ budget price ££ mid-range price £££ expensive £££+ most expensive

▶ *The Copenhagen Botanical Gardens' glasshouse and pond*

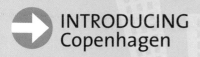

INTRODUCING
Copenhagen

Introduction

Dynamic yet quaint. Small and compact, yet complex and rich.
Pedestrianised streets, wide, ancient city squares and festivals
galore. Copenhagen, Denmark's capital and arguably Scandinavia's
liveliest city, will keep you entertained all year round.

You'll immediately notice how laid-back the people of Copenhagen
are. The locals love to enjoy life, so there are countless cafés and bars,
numerous well-kept parks, and vibrant harbour and beach areas.
It is a happy city, comfortable with itself and its place in the world.

It is a clean, healthy city to visit, too. A car is the last thing you
will want, as you can walk from one area to another in half an hour.
You can hire a bike and spin around with the rest of the eco-friendly
inhabitants. If that is too energetic, you can hop on the speedy and
efficient designer metro.

Culture and design are two of Copenhagen's finest qualities.
You'll see cutting-edge displays of architectural, interior and fashion
design, both ancient and modern, thanks in part to Denmark's royal
family, the Carlsberg Foundation and the city's other illustrious
benefactors.

Cuisine is also big, with nine restaurants boasting Michelin stars. Top-
quality international food is mingled with hearty Danish specialities.

Music is everywhere in this fun-loving city, and there are regular
live performances from local talents and big names. Don't miss the
popular annual Jazz Festival (see pages 12–13).

And there is mindless pleasure too. If that is your thing, come to
the Tivoli Gardens, a little 21st-century Eden where all is well in the
world. You'll find computer games alongside giant puppets, stomach-
churning rides beside kitsch merry-go-rounds. Here, Hans Christian
Andersen's well-loved fairy stories have no darker side.

But whatever you do in Copenhagen, you'll have to try hard for your visit, like a fairy story, not to end happily ever after.

● *Hans Christian Andersen Statue on Rådhuspladsen*

When to go

Summer days in Copenhagen are long and bright, and winter evenings can be long and dark. Summer is the time when Copenhageners leave the city and foreign visitors flock to it, for the host of festivals, entertainment and events around the harbour and canals. Some sights may close during winter. Come for the Christmas market, though, when the city is lit up and has a warm, magical spirit, in spite of the cooler temperatures.

SEASONS & CLIMATE

Winters are a few degrees colder than in Britain, but still relatively mild. Snow rarely arrives now before February or March.

Spring is either very short, or lasts the whole summer. Spring is chilly but bright, and the driest time of year. The temperature in summer peaks at around 30°C (86°F), but it rains more, and can be humid. Towards September expect mild sunny days.

Autumn barely happens, and by November the temperature is back to single figures. Be warned that the temperature in winter is unpredictable, and frequently fluctuates more than 10°C (50°F) in one day.

ANNUAL EVENTS

January
New Year Celebrations in Rådhuspladsen and firework displays all over town. Lots of concerts leading up to midnight.

February–March
Copenhagen Catwalk Fashion shows and events on catwalks, in shops and on the streets, late Mar–early Apr. Ⓦ www.copenhagencatwalk.com Ⓔ info@copenhagencatwalk.com

Dyrehavsbakken (Bakken Amusement Park) officially opens for the year the last Thursday in March. Hundreds of motorcyclists congregate in Nørrebro and head out to Bakken in convoy. ➋ Dyrehavsbakken, Klampenborg ❶ 39633544 ❿ www.bakken.dk ❺ bakken@bakken.dk

Natfilm Festival Ten days of Danish and international films in late Mar. Including re-runs, old movies and previews. ❶ 33120005 ❿ www.natfilm.dk ❺ info@natfilm.dk

April–May

Queen Margrethe II's birthday The Queen appears on the balcony at Amalienborg Slot at noon on 16 Apr and the Royal Guard parades in ceremonial uniform.

⬤ *Amalienborg Palace*

Tivoli Gardens opens for the summer season. Ⓦ www.tivoli.dk
May Day Parade to Fælled Park by trade unionists and workers. Speeches, music events, food stalls and lots of ale.
Copenhagen Architecture and Design Days (Cph ADD) Events and exhibitions throughout the city over three days in early May. Ⓦ www.cphadd.com Ⓔ info@cphadd.com
Ølfestival (Beer festival) over three days at Valby Hallen. Ⓦ www.ale.dk
Copenhagen Marathon Over 26 years old, the Copenhagen marathon circles the city on a Sunday in mid-May. Ⓦ www.copenhagenmarathon.dk Ⓔ info@copenhagenmarathon.dk

June–July
Whitsun Carnival Parade from Strøget to Fælledparken. Three days of Latin American fun and world music. Ⓦ www.karneval.dk
Sankt Hans Aften The longest day of the year is 23 June. Bonfires and parties on the beaches and in the parks.
Roskilde Festival Rock festival with 70,000 or more visitors, big names, stalls, camping, mud and chemical toilets. Late June–July. Ⓐ Dyrskuepladsen, Darupvej Ⓣ 46366613 Ⓦ www.roskilde-festival.dk Ⓔ info@roskilde-festival.dk
Jazz Festival Ten days of indoor and outdoor performances around the city (see pages 12–13).

August–October
Copenhagen Pride Week Gay pride parade and a week of events in mid-Aug. Ⓦ www.copenhagenpride.dk
Copenhagen Film Festival End of Sept. Ⓐ Goethersgade 175 Ⓣ 33454749 Ⓦ www.copenhagenfilmfestival.com Ⓔ info@copenhagenfilmfestival.com

Cultural Night Museums, theatres and galleries are open late and free of charge on the first night of the school autumn term. Ⓦ www.kulturnatten.dk
Copenhagen Cooking (Nordic Food Festival) Scandinavia's largest food festival. Special menu at selected restaurants. Late Aug–early Sept. Ⓦ www.copenhagencooking.dk

November–December
Copenhagen Autumn Jazz in clubs throughout the city, early Nov.
Ⓣ 33932013 Ⓦ www.jazzfestival.dk
Christmas Parade to light the tree in Rådhuspladsen, last Sat in Nov.
Ⓦ www.visitcopenhagen.com
Tivoli Christmas Market Christmas shopping, ice skating, good eating and a glass of *gløgg* (mulled wine). Mid-Nov–Christmas. Ⓦ www.tivoli.dk

PUBLIC HOLIDAYS
Nytårs dag (New Year's Day) 1 Jan
Skærtorsdag, Langfredag, 2 Påskedag (Maundy Thursday, Good Friday & Easter Monday) 20, 21 & 24 March 2008; 9, 10 & 13 April 2009
Stor Bededag (Common Prayer Day) Fourth Friday after Good Friday
Kristi himmelfartsdag (Ascension Day) 22 May 2008; 11 June 2009
2 Pinsedag (Whit Monday) 12 June 2008; 1 June 2009
Grundlovsdag (Constitution Day) 5 June
Juleferie (Christmas) 24–26 Dec

Public transport runs to Sunday schedules, and banks, post offices and public buildings are closed on these days. Except on Constitution Day, most shops, but not restaurants, will also be closed.

The Jazz Festival

Copenhagen's most celebrated event is the annual Jazz Festival, a local institution since 1978. It takes place over ten days in July, starting on the first Friday. Whether you're a jazz enthusiast, or someone who likes to hear it in the background at a trendy bar, don't miss this event.

During the festival, every possible space in the city becomes a venue. The Tivoli Gardens and the Royal Theatre are where the big names play, but cafés, parks, clubs, public squares, churches, the canal banks and museums are a stage for the hundreds of talented performers who flock here. You will hear all kinds of jazz, from traditional to experimental.

The big concerts can be expensive, but they're worth it. Cafés and clubs only charge a small entrance fee, and open-air events are free. Some of the best small performances are those by Denmark's home-grown jazz musicians.

The rich history of jazz in Copenhagen adds a telling dimension. During World War II, the music became a form of resistance to the German occupation. In the 1960s, the great American jazz musicians heard about Denmark's reputation for liberality and permissiveness and found their way here. Some of them made it their home, and perhaps this explains the quality and intensity of local talent as well as the enthusiasm of those who listen to it

Household names – Dizzie Gillespie, Ray Charles, Ella Fitzgerald, Oscar Peterson, Winton Marsalis – have played here. Future household names are still coming. The festival hosts top American, Brazilian, Argentinean, Austrian and Scandinavian artists, and proudly showcases an extensive line-up of local talent.

Copenhagen is a wonderful place to be in summer anyway. But the Jazz Festival takes life out onto the streets, and a sunny, laughing, relaxed chaos hits the city. The music and atmosphere have become so popular that the city now holds another festival, Autumn Jazz, in early November.

The city's accommodation gets packed during the festival, so make sure you book early.

Copenhagen Jazz Festival ⊕ Nytorv 3 ⊕ 33932013 ⊕ www.jazzfestival.dk

⬆ July sees jazz all over the city – afloat, on the streets, wherever there's space

History

Like all fairytale heroes, Copenhagen had humble beginnings. In the 12th century it was just a scruffy hamlet called Havn, surrounded on all sides by salt marshes and reliant upon fishing for trade. The dominant city in Denmark was Roskilde (see pages 126–33), with its stone cathedral and kings.

It was piracy that gave Copenhagen its break. In 1167 King Valdemar I sent his brother Bishop Absalon to sort out pirates who were attacking shipping in the area. Havn's strategic position was perfect for controlling the Øresund, Denmark's narrow shipping channel, and Bishop Absalon quickly built a fortress there. Thus Copenhagen was founded.

The city's growth has been turbulent. A couple of centuries after its foundation, Copenhagen's *Köbmandshavn* (merchant's harbour), was being attacked regularly by its neighbours for its strategic importance. In 1443 the Danish kings moved their capital there. In 1536, during the peasants' revolt, Copenhagen was besieged. The city's residents ate rats for a while, then gave this up and surrendered quickly to the king's forces. In the same year, Denmark broke away from the Roman Catholic church.

It was only in the 16th century that Christian IV began the first proper building projects, such as Christianshavn (see pages 90–103), the Rundetårn, the Børsen, old stock exchange (see pages 90–2), and Rosenborg Slot (Rosenborg Castle) (see page 108). A lot of the city was subsequently destroyed by a fire in 1728 and a 30-year war with its neighbours. A plague wiped out 20,000 inhabitants of the city around the same time. Copenhagen didn't have it easy.

It didn't get much better in the 19th century when there was another seige, this time by Admiral Lord Nelson. A fledgling cultural renaissance, centred around the writer Hans Christian Andersen, the philosopher Søren Kierkegaard and the sculptor Thorvaldsen, was overcome by the industrial revolution which hit Copenhagen at the same time. Workers flocked to the city, poverty and squalor increased, and Vesterbro and Nørrebro were created as workers' homes.

In 1940 Germany invaded. Five years of occupation followed, but Denmark, uniquely in Europe, managed to rescue the vast majority of its Jews.

The war marked a turning point in Copenhagen's economic and social history. A nationwide social welfare programme was instituted, and in the 1960s Denmark boomed. Immigrant workers rushed to take up new employment opportunities. The first skyscraper, the Radisson Hotel, went up. Copenhagen's youth joined protests about the nuclear bomb, Vietnam and education. Pornography was legalised.

The 1970s saw the establishment of the free state of Christiania (see pages 92–3) in a disused army base, and Denmark joined the European Economic Community. In 2000 the building of the Øresund Bridge linked Copenhagen with Sweden by road and rail, reinforcing its position as an economic and social power. A conservative government and some religious tensions have recently challenged Denmark's celebrated tradition of openness and acceptance. But if history teaches us anything, it is that Copenhagen's future will be anything but dull and predictable.

🔺 *Early Danish headgear, National Museum*

Lifestyle

Copenhagen's history helps us to understand the lifestyle and attitudes of its people today. It hasn't been a cheerful and easy one, with its pirates, fires, plagues, sieges, occupations and unrest. Now Copenhageners want a bit of law and order. For a simple yet telling example, look out for their quasi-religious obedience of pedestrian crossing signals.

The anarchy which used to exist in the heart of the city is slowly being phased out, and Copenhagen is moving into the 21st century. Christiania displays this transformation in action. On the one hand, Christiania is a genuinely anarchist society, run along democratic lines. Crime is kept low not by the law but by cooperation between the residents. The community pays little or nothing in rent and taxes, and looks after itself happily. Young people spend their weekends enjoying the atmosphere. On the other hand, Christiania is prime real estate, and several successful businesses are already established

SOCIAL ETIQUETTE

Copenhagen's social rules spring from a paradoxical mixture of respect for law and order, and democratic anarchy. Here are a couple of tips.

Obey pedestrian crossing signals and keep out of cycle lanes. Observe every British rule about queuing, except, oddly, at bus stops. It's best not to offend residents by taking photographs in Christiania, as if it's a tourist attraction. And remember that everyone is equal in Copenhagen. Don't expect waiters or cleaners to grovel.

there. The fascinating social experiment it represents won't last all that long. So visit now (see pages 92–3).

Law, order, anarchy and, more importantly, *hygge*. This is a specifically Danish concept, meaning 'cosiness' or 'togetherness'. It conjures up the idea of keeping the forces of darkness at bay with good cheer, of social responsibility and looking after one another. On a political level, Denmark's great social welfare system sums this up. On a social level, see it everywhere at Tivoli (see pages 82–3) and during the Jazz Festival (see pages 12–13).

▲ *A couple having a heart-to-heart at the Three Lakes*

Culture

Copenhagen arguably leads the world in interior design. Perhaps that is not surprising. *Hygge*, or 'cosiness' (see Lifestyle section), also means the need to create a secure and happy environment.

As you'll see, Danish furniture, cutlery and other home furnishings manage to combine form with function. The well-known Danish egg chair, for example, provides ultimate comfort with a simple, flowing grace. Arne Jacobsen's smooth steel teapots are beautiful to look at, and don't dribble tea. The silversmith Georg Jensen has produced beautiful silver pieces of jewellery and silverware along similar flowing lines. Nowadays Danish design is still thriving, particularly in Copenhagen, with shops all over selling fine glassware and lamps, furniture and other home furnishings.

The country has other cultural highs too, in music, literature, theatre, arts and cinema. Copenhagen, as its vibrant capital, has the best of them all.

As well as hosting two of the best rock and jazz festivals in Europe, the city has a lively traditional classical music scene. Resident orchestras include the Zealand Symphony Orchestra and the Danish Radio Symphony Orchestra. A new opera house opened in 2005. On a day in mid-August there are free open-air performances in **Fælledparken** ❸ Øster Allé 35 Ⓦ www.kgl-teater.dk

Theatre is both conservative and avante-garde. Det Kongelige Teater (the Royal Theatre, see page 64) is a popular theatre and also the home of the Danish Royal Ballet Company. The London Toast Theatre (see page 30) puts on light comedies in English.

◗ *Humble items but great design at the Dansk Design Center*

▲ *Cutting edge design for the new Copenhagen Opera House*

Cinema has a long history in Denmark and has been undergoing a quiet revival in recent years. Don't miss the popular new international film festival in September (see page 10).

▶ *Strøget is Denmark's, and Europe's, longest pedestrianised shopping street*

Shopping

Thankfully, Copenhagen isn't filled with cheap, tacky souvenirs. But it is the place to spend time and money finding something valuable.

Danish design is everywhere, in everyday items such as cutlery, pots and pans, table lamps and clothes. Try shops such as Illums Bolighus, Georg Jensen and Royal Copenhagen on the main shopping street Strøget. Go for some Arne Jacobsen-designed steel items such as his ashtray, coffee pot or vacuum flask. Royal Copenhagen porcelain (ⓦ www.royalcopenhagen.com) is very collectible. Georg Jensen shops sell inventive and original jewellery. For clothes, you'll find the city is full of boutiques and vintage clothes shops with designs and sizes to suit all tastes.

Choose the perfect gift for children from hundreds of cut paper mobiles, many featuring events from Hans Christian Andersen stories. And if you go at the right time of year, Copenhagen sells the best Christmas decorations in Europe.

Strøget and the surrounding streets are the best places to start shopping, while the pedestrianised streets of Nørrebro have lots of funky clothes, antiques and design shops. Istegade is the place for

SHOPPING HOURS

Shops generally open on weekdays around 10.00–10.30 and close between 17.00 and 19.00, sometimes 20.00 on Friday. On Saturdays, most places except large department stores close between 14.00 and 15.00. Almost everywhere is closed on Sunday. On the first Saturday and Sunday of the month, however, shops all open until around 18.00.

USEFUL SHOPPING PHRASES

What time does the shop open/close?
Hvornår åbner/lukker butikken?
Vohnor orbna/lorka boo-teeken?

How much is this?
Hvor meget koster det?
Vohr mah-eht kosta di?

I'd like to buy it
Jeg vil gerne købe det
Yai vi gairneh hay di

This is too large/too small. Do you have any others?
Den er for stor/lille. Har du andre?
Dehn air fo store/lilla. Hah do andera?

fetish gear and trendy shoe and clothes shops. Bredgade is known for upmarket design and antiques.

Christiania is worth browsing for young, trendy presents, while Islands Brygge is great for kooky clothes by local designers. Take a wander down Gammel Kongevej for more designer clothing, organic food stores and classic Scandinavian interior design shops. Copenhagen also has several excellent weekend flea markets.

Eating & drinking

Whether you just want a quick snack or a light lunch, whether you prefer to spend the evening over a beer and a good dinner, or whether you fancy treating yourself to a luxurious six-course haute cuisine piece of culinary art, there is something for you in Copenhagen. Nine restaurants boasting Michelin stars is a lot for a small city, and there are many more great establishments at the cutting edge of Danish fusion cooking.

Traditional Danish cuisine is mostly based on meat, in particular pork, beef and duck. Venison often appears on the menu. Fish is popular, especially pollock, hake, mackerel and herring, and dishes are usually

served with potatoes and root vegetables. Danes enjoy dense, dark bread and a wide variety of cheeses. *Smørrebrød* is an open sandwich traditionally made with rye or wheat bread and piled high with cold meats or herring, garnished with pickled vegetables or salad.

Eating out in Copenhagen's luxury restaurants is not cheap, but it's a real treat. Often, they serve a fusion of French and Danish kitchen, blending traditional Danish ingredients with French specialities such as foie gras. Some unusual foods appear on your plate in the very upmarket restaurants – chickweed or nasturtium flowers, for example.

Enjoy the harbour view and Opera House from your table at Custom House

PRICE CATEGORIES

Based on the average price per head for a three-course dinner, excluding drinks. Lunch will usually be a little cheaper in each category.

£ up to 250kr ££ 250–400kr £££ over 400kr

Fortunately for your wallet, cheap, good, fun places serving hearty, well-cooked food abound. Café bars offer loaded sandwiches, burgers and often a daily pasta or wok dish. Ethnic restaurants have taken off, especially in Nørrebro and Vesterbro. Thai restaurants and sushi bars are popular.

European cafés are everywhere, and many have their own specialities in food, cocktails, wine, coffee, music, interior design, or art. Most of them are open until around midnight, but stop serving food between 21.00 and 22.00. In *smørrebrød* bars you can enjoy a traditional open sandwich.

If you want to have a meal in one of the parks, or by the harbour or beachside, you can get great meals to go from many cafés, authentic Italian pizzerias and the top-class delis which are popping up in Vesterbro, Nørrebro, Frederiksberg and Christianshavn. Or you can make your own. All over the city there are good delicatessens and supermarkets where you can buy bread, cheese, cold meats and pickles, and bakeries selling hot bread, *wienerbrød* (Danish pastries), filled sandwiches and coffee.

The Danes have a strong beer culture, and locally brewed beers are popular. Wine lists in restaurants are impressive, but often expensive. One traditional drink to try when eating a *smørrebrød*, is *akvavit*, an astringent liqueur which is thrown down as quickly as

USEFUL DINING PHRASES

I would like a table for ... people, please
Et bord til ..., tak
It boorr ti ..., tack

I am a vegetarian
Jeg er vegetar
Yai air veggehtar

Where is the toilet (restroom) please?
Hvor er toilettet, tak?
Vohr air toylehdeht, tack?

May I have the bill, please?
Jeg vil gerne betale regningen?
Yai vi gairneh bitaileh rhiningehn?

Do you accept credit cards?
Tager I kreditkort?
Tah ee krehdeetkort?

possible and followed by a beer chaser. For an after-dinner *digestif*, try *Gammel Dansk* (Old Danish).

There is no need to leave elaborate tips. It is usual to round up the bill to the nearest 10kr or leave 10 or 20kr for the waiter. Your credit card receipt will usually have a space for you to write in a tip if you wish.

Entertainment & nightlife

CLUBS

Like its range of restaurants, Copenhagen's club scene has grown to match its increasing wealth and its ethnic and libertarian influences. Most musical tastes are catered to and clubs and discos exist to suit every lifestyle, wallet and age group.

Some of Copenhagen's café bars metamorphose at night into clubs, and some clubs open during the day. Most clubs go in and out of fashion, but places such as **Vega** (ⓐ Enghavevej 40 ❶ 33257011 ⓦ www.vega.dk) are still going strong after many years. Vega, indeed, receives government subsidies.

Clubs get going quite late, especially at weekends when they are empty until well past 01.00. This may be because drinking all night and into the early hours would be prohibitively expensive. Many clubs have a lower age limit of 21. Check out ⓦ www.aok.dk for details of what's on.

LIVE MUSIC

Major venues for classical musical performances include:
Christianskirke ⓐ Strandgade 2 ❶ 32541576 ⓦ www.christianskirke.dk
Holmens Kirke (Navy Church) gives regular concerts and special performances at Easter and Christmas (see pages 96–7).
Det Kongelige Teater (see page 64).
Radiohusets Koncertsal, the home of the Danish National Symphony Orchestra gives live performances every Thursday.
ⓐ Julius Thomsens Gade 1 ❶ 35206262
Den Sorte Diamant (The Black Diamond) (see page 98).
Tivolis Koncertsal ⓐTietensgade ❶ 33151012 ⓦ www.tivoli.dk

ENTERTAINMENT & NIGHTLIFE ✓

DANCE

Copenhagen has a lively modern dance scene, with more than ten small dance companies. Look out for work by:

Åben Dans Production Presents contemporary pieces, often using improvised movement, to live concert performances.
🄰 Hørsholmsgade 20 ☎ 35820610 🆆 www.aabendans.dk
🄴 mail@aabendans.dk

Peter Schaufuss Ballet Influential award-winning choreographer in European modern dance. ☎ 97405122 🆆 www.schaufuss.com

Venues for modern dance include:
Dansescenen 🄰 Østerfælled Torv 34 ☎ 35438300/35432021
🆆 www.dansescenen.dk 🄴 info@dansescenen.dk
Kanonhallen 🄰 Kigurren 1–3 ☎ 35432324 🆆 www.kanonhallen.net
Tivoli (see pages 82–3).

CINEMA

Copenhagen has cinema from multiplex to art house. Films are shown in the original language and subtitled in Danish, and you can take alcohol in with you.

Cinemaxx 🄰 Fisketorvet Shopping Centre, Kalvebod Brygge
☎ 70101202 🆆 www.cinemaxx.dk 🄴 koebenhavn@cinemaxx.dk
Empire Bio 🄰 Guldbergsgade 29f ☎ 35360036 🆆 www.empirebio.dk
Gloria 🄰 Rådhuspladsen 59 ☎ 33124292 🆆 www.gloria.dk
🄴 info@gloria.dk
Grand Teatret 🄰 Mikkel Bryggers Gade 8 ☎ 33151611
🆆 www.grandteatret.dk
Palads 🄰 Axeltorv 9 ☎ 70131211 🆆 www.biobooking.dk
Park Bio 🄰 Østerbrogade 79 ☎ 35383362 🆆 www.parkbio-kbh.dk

● *Det Kongelige Teater at Kongens Nytorv*

THEATRE

Most theatre in Copenhagen is in Danish, but for English performances try:

London Toast Theatre ⓐ Kochsvej 18 ⓣ 33228686
ⓦ www.londontoast.dk

That Theatre Company ⓐ Axeltorv 12 ⓣ 33135042 ⓦ www.that-theatre.com ⓔ info@that-theatre.com

LISTINGS & TICKETS

The English-language weekly newspaper *Copenhagen Post* has information about performances and events in the city. Find free copies in cafés and shops or purchase it in newsagents, or check Ⓦ www.cphpost.dk. *Copenhagen This Week* is a free monthly publication containing events listings. Ⓦ www.ctw.dk

Billetlugen sells tickets on-line and at any of the FONA (electrical) stores. Ⓦ www.billetlugen.dk

Billetnet sells tickets on-line, by telephone, and at any post office. ❶ 38481122 Ⓦ www.billetnet.dk

E-Billet, for e-tickets to some concerts and cinemas Ⓦ www.e-billet.dk

Tivoli Billetcenter at the entrance to Tivoli Gardens sells tickets for Tivoli and other events. ❷ Vesterbrogade 3 ❶ 33151012 ❹ 09.00–20.00 when Tivoli is open

Sport & relaxation

Sport and sport facilities in Denmark are open to all. As well as football and handball, there are several swimming pools and fitness centres, plus plenty of opportunities for golf, skating, riding, tennis and more.

SPECTATOR SPORTS
Football
Played from late July–Nov and Mar–early June. There are two main teams playing at different stadiums.

Brøndby IF tickets cost 110–220kr. **ⓐ** Brøndby Stadion 30, Brøndby **ⓣ** 39692345 **ⓦ** www.brondby.com

FC København (National Stadium) tickets cost 80–200kr from Billetlugen (see page 31), more for international games. **ⓐ** Parken, Øster Allé 50 **ⓣ** 35437400 **ⓦ** www.fck.dk **ⓔ** info@fck.dk

Handball
Ajax Farun **ⓐ** Bavnehøj Hallen, Enghavevej 90 **ⓣ** 33214900 **ⓦ** www.dhf.dk

Ice hockey
Rungsted Cobras season runs Nov–Mar. **ⓐ** Stadionallé 11, Rungsted Kyst **ⓣ** 45763031 **ⓦ** www.rik.dk

PARTICIPATION SPORTS
Ice skating
Winter is the time for ice skating in Copenhagen, with outdoor rinks set up around the city in Kongens Nytorv, Tivoli, Blågårdsplads and several other locations. There is an indoor skating rink at **Østerbro Skøjtehal** **ⓐ** Per Henrik Lings Allé 6 **ⓣ** 35421865 **ⓛ** 12.00–14.45 Mon–Fri, 16.00–18.30 Sun, closed Sat

Jogging

Joggers use most of the parks in the city as well as the Three Lakes and the harbour area between Langebro Bridge and Fisketorv shopping centre. It is safe to jog alone at sensible times and when other people are around.

Sports & fitness centres

DGI-Byen Family-friendly, modern sports centre with courts for ball games, an enormous pool, a bowling alley and spa facilities.
🅐 Tietensgade 63 ❶ 33298000 Ⓦ www.dgi-byen.dk 🕐 06.30–24.00 Mon–Thur, 06.30–01.00 Fri, 09.00–20.00 Sat & Sun (opening hours vary)
Fitness dk Denmark's largest fitness centre chain found at numerous locations in Copenhagen. ❶ 33432800 Ⓦ www.fitnessdk.dk
SATS A chain of fitness centres located throughout the city.
❶ 33321002 Ⓦ www.sats.com

Swimming

For indoor swimming try **DGI-Byen** (see above) and the recently renovated **Frederiksberg Svømmehal** with spa facilities and child-friendly pools.
🅐 Helgesvej 29 ❶ 38140400 Ⓦ www.frederiksbergsvoemmehal.dk
For outdoor swimming try one of Copenhagen's two Havnebad (harbour bathing areas) also known as Copacabana:
Havnebadet ved Fisketorvet is made up of several floating bridges and contains three bathing areas: one for kids, one for serious swimmers, and one diving pool. 🅐 Havneholmen ❶ 23710185 Ⓦ www.islands-brygge.com 🕐 11.00–19.00 June–Aug
Islands Brygge Havnebad has five swimming areas: two for kids, two 50 m (164 ft) pools, and one diving pool. If you don't feel like swimming then just relax in the sun with the other visitors to Islands Brygge.
🅐 Islands Brygge ❶ 23713189 Ⓦ www.islands-brygge.com
🕐 07.00–19.00 Mon–Fri, 11.00–19.00 Sat & Sun, June–Aug

Accommodation

The main accommodation areas are around Central Station, Nyhavn and Nørreport. The number of hotel rooms in Copenhagen has more than doubled since 1999 and the city's accommodation is becoming known for its state-of-the-art-design. Accommodation for all budgets can be found in hotels, self-catering apartments, youth hostels and B&Bs within the city, and in campsites, manor houses and guesthouses outside the city. The usual 1- to 5-star rating system applies.

Turning up in Copenhagen without a reservation can be risky, as during the summer and well into September rooms are usually fully booked. In the off season, though, you can try bargaining for reduced rates with receptionists, or find good deals through the booking agency in Copenhagen Right Now (see page 150).

Prices for rooms in B&Bs are between 280 and 550kr per night and can be found through **Dansk Bed & Breakfast** ⓐ Sankt Peders Stræde 41 ❶ 39610405 ⓦ www.bbdk.dk ⓔ bed@bbdk.dk

For general accommodation information and listings ⓐ Gammel Kongevej 1 ❶ 33257400 ⓦ www.visitcopenhagen.com

PRICE CATEGORIES
Based on the average cost of a double room in the high season.
£ up to 600kr ££ 600–900kr £££ 900–1,200kr £££+ over 1,200kr

HOTELS
Rådhuspladsen & the West

Cab Inn City £ Central and clean, but with tiny rooms. Lounge area, 24-hour reception, helpful staff. See also its sister hotels Cab Inn Scandinavia or Cab Inn Copenhagen, both in Frederiksberg.
🄰 Mitchellsgade 14 ☎ 33461616 🔵 www.cabinn.com

Hotel Selandia £–£££ Central and popular, with comfortable newly renovated rooms and free wireless internet. 🄰 Helgolandsgade 12 ☎ 33314610 🔵 www.hotel-selandia.dk

The Square £££ New hotel located on town hall square. Stylishly decorated rooms and great breakfast, with a view over the city. 🄰 Rådhuspladsen 14 ☎ 33381200 🔵 www.thesquare.dk 🄴 thesquare@arp-hansen.dk

Hotel Alexandra £££+ Design hotel with individually furnished rooms and pieces from several of Denmark's most famous designers. Environmentally friendly, with an allergy-friendly floor and organic breakfast buffet. Adjoining brasserie. 🄰 H C Andersens Boulevard 8 ☎ 33744444 🔵 www.hotel-alexandra.dk

Radisson SAS Royal Hotel £££+ Skyscraper designed in its entirety by Arne Jacobsen. Amazing views, comfortable rooms and egg chairs. 🄰 Hammerichsgade 1 ☎ 33426000 🔵 www.radisson.com

Nyhavn area
Sømandshjemmet Bethel ££ Former seaman's hostel. 🄰 Nyhavn 22 ☎ 33130370 🔵 www.hotel-bethel.dk 🄴 info@hotel-bethel.dk

● *Hotel Alexandra, a design-conscious hotel in a design-conscious city*

Hotel Maritime £££–£££+ Quiet location close to Nyhavn and the harbour with small but well-equipped rooms and a pleasant lounge area. ● Peder Skrams Gade 19 ● 33134882 ● www.hotel-maritime.dk ● hotel@maritime.dk

Hotel Opera £££+ In a quiet street behind Det Kongelige Teater. Charming, British-inspired with good atmosphere. ● Tordenskjoldsgade 15 ● 33478300 ● www.hotelopera.dk

71 Nyhavn £££+ Beautifully renovated 200-year-old warehouse. Ancient beams, luxurious suites and some lovely views over the harbour. Good restaurant. ● Nyhavn 71 ● 33436200 ● www.71nyhavnhotel.dk

Around the Three Lakes

Hotel Jørgensen ££ Simply furnished, spotless rooms.
Dormitory accommodation also available. ⓐ Rømersgade 11
ⓣ 33138186 ⓦ www.hoteljoergensen.dk ⓔ hoteljoergensen@mail.dk

Hotel Nora ££ Old apartment block on the Nørrebro side of the
lakes. ⓐ Nørrebrogade 18b ⓣ 35372021 ⓦ www.hotelnora.dk
ⓔ nora@hotelnora.dk

Hotel Fox £££ Individually designed rooms, fabulous buffet
breakfast, rooftop terrace and a great lounge with café and bar.
ⓐ Jarmers Plads 3 ⓣ 33133000 ⓦ www.hotelfox.dk
ⓔ hotel@hotelfox.dk

Ibsens Hotel £££ Converted period building, with rooms built into
the original structures. Free hot drinks and internet in lounge.
ⓐ Vendersgade 23 ⓣ 33131913 ⓦ www.hotel@ibsenshotel.dk
ⓔ hotel@ibsenhotel.dk

HOSTELS & SLEEP-INNS

Some hostels have en suite twin rooms, but most are summer-only
dormitories. A dormitory bed costs around 80–120kr.

City Public Hostel £ Dormitory only, near Central Station. Open
24 hours; bed linen and breakfast extra, free wireless internet
access, kitchen and barbeque. ⓐ Absalonsgade 8 ⓣ 33312070
ⓦ www.citypublichostel.dk ⓔ info@citypublichostel.dk

Sleep-in Green £ Small, ecologically sound hostel open summer only in Nørrebro. ⓐ Ravnsborggade 18 ❶ 35377777 ⓦ www.sleep-in-green.dk

Sleep in Heaven £ Backpacker spot with free internet access and chillout room. ⓐ Struensegade 7 ❶ 35354648 ⓦ www.sleepinheaven.com ⓔ morefun@sleepinheaven.com

Danhostel Copenhagen City £–££ The first designer hostel in Europe offering spotlessly clean and modern dorms and private rooms. ⓐ H C Andersen Boulevard 50 ❶ 33188332 ⓦ www.danhostel.dk ⓔ cphcitybooking@danhostel.dk

⭕ *Arne Jacobsen design plus unbeatable views at the Royal*

THE BEST OF COPENHAGEN

The longer you can spend in Copenhagen, the better. Even when you have sampled the full variety of sights, museums, shops and other delights that the city offers, there's still plenty to see and do in the surrounding area of North Zealand, easily accessible by local train and bus.

A canal cruise is the best way to get an overview of the most picturesque and unique parts of the city. Try **DFDS Canal Tours** ⓐ Gammel Strand 26 ❶ 33423320 ⓦ www.canaltours.com ⓛ 10.00–17.00 (summer); 09.55–14.55 (winter)

For the best attractions for children, see pages 146–8.

TOP 10 ATTRACTIONS

- **Tivoli Gardens** An evening of pure fun and pleasure, ending, on Wednesdays and Saturdays, with a firework display (see pages 82–3)

- **Ny Carlsberg Glyptotek (Carlsberg Sculpture Centre)** Enjoy a coffee in the winter gardens surrounded by stunning sculptures (see pages 85–6)

- **Christiania** A stroll through a unique social experiment (see pages 92–3)

- **Assistens Kirkegård** The most beautiful garden in Copenhagen. Visit Hans Christian Andersen in his place of rest (see page 44)

- **Canal boat cruise** Take a waterborne tour around the city (see opposite)

- *Smørrebrød* Danish speciality, best enjoyed in a traditional city centre café (see page 25)

- **Shopping** in the side streets around Strøget (see page 67)

- **Rosenborg Slot** Admire the crown jewels (see page 108)

- **Vor Frelsers Kirke (Church of Our Saviour)** For the thrill of the climb and the views from the top (see pages 98–9)

- **Roskilde** A trip to see Denmark's old capital and authentic Viking ships (see pages 126–33)

🔽 *Detail of a carousel in amusement park Tivoli*

Suggested itineraries

HALF-DAY: COPENHAGEN IN A HURRY

If you're just passing through or snatching some free time on
a business trip and only have a morning or an afternoon – where
do you go? Art lovers must seek out the Statens Museum for Kunst
(National Gallery) (see page 112) while pleasure seekers should head
straight for the canal tour – sit down and see the lot at the same
time, if only from canal level. Anarchists will want to go to Christiania
and beer lovers will be torn between the Carlsberg Visitor Centre
and a long lunch or dinner at Nørrebro Bryghus (see page 114).

1 DAY: TIME TO SEE A LITTLE MORE

Start your day with the Danish breakfast – Danish pastries, croissants,
black bread and mild Danish cheese and fresh fruit, perhaps in the
Radisson (see page 80) where you can simultaneously admire some
of Denmark's most famous exports – the egg chair, swan chair and
coffee pots by Arne Jacobsen. Fill your morning with one of the half-
day suggestions, and maybe your afternoon with one of the others.

    Alternatively, stroll over to Strøget, shop your way down to Kongens
Nytorv and lunch at Nyhavn, where you can choose one of the Nyhavnside
cafés. In the afternoon head down Gothersgade towards Nørreport
where the afternoon can be whiled away in Kongens Have, or the
Botanical Gardens or Rosenberg Slot, admiring the crown jewels,
wondering why anyone would want cutlery made of glass. Your evening
should start with a classy meal, perhaps in L'Education Nationale or in
the famed, and rather more expensive, Noma, both serving the best
French and Danish combination in the city. After dinner head over to
Tivoli for a ride or just wander about catching the performances and the
sound and light show or (if it's Wednesday or Saturday) the fireworks.

2–3 DAYS: TIME TO SEE MUCH MORE

With a couple more days Slotsholmen would take up a morning, doing the tour of the royal residence, admiring the Black Diamond and perhaps picnicking in the Royal Library Gardens. The afternoon should be dedicated to some serious culture, perhaps the Statens Museum for Kunst, or the Nationalmuseet (National Museum). Dinner at Custom House (see page 74) followed by a performance at the opera house, arriving by water taxi would round out the highbrow evening or you could go on to one of the city's clubs which are just getting started around 01.00. Save your serious shopping for your second or third morning, checking out some of the trendier shops in Nørrebro and Frederiksberg but spend the afternoon in Christiania, a place like nowhere else. If you like it stay for the evening – there's usually music of some kind going on, or just hang out in a bar. Otherwise one of the canalside restaurants, say Kanalen (page 103) would make a pleasantly romantic evening, followed by a stroll back to the city centre and a late-night bar somewhere behind Illum department store.

LONGER: ENJOYING COPENHAGEN TO THE FULL

On a longer stay you ought to visit some of the smaller art collections, spend an afternoon strolling along the harbour to Amalienborg to see the Queen's winter residence, then on to the Gefion Fountain, the English Church and the Little Mermaid. A week would allow a day trip to Roskilde to visit the Viking Ship Museum and one to Helsingør to see the castle Hamlet never lived in. You could easily while away half a day viewing art and lunching at Louisiana – art in a garden. In the evenings there are movies, the theatre and some good clubs and in between there's always shopping.

Something for nothing

There are lots of other things you can do in Copenhagen which are completely free. Most of Copenhagen's museums have free entrance on Wednesdays. All of the churches are free and there are plenty of architectural and design wonders to be seen among them. Be sure to visit Vor Frelsers Kirke in Christianshavn with its beautiful golden spiral steeple. The magnificent **Grundtvigs Kirke** just outside the Nørrebro district in Norvest (❸ På Bjerget 14b) was designed by the influential lighting and furniture designer Kaare Jensen-Klint, and his father.

Some of the libraries are also worth a visit. As well as The Black Diamond (see page 98) pop into the University Library on Fiolstræde, which has a beautifully kept wooden interior and delightful ceilings.

All of the parks have a unique layout and offer something special. A less likely place to relax, but one that is well used by joggers, sunbathers and picnickers is the beautiful Assistens Kirkegård, which is in fact a cemetery. As well as some of Denmark's most famous deceased, it contains a wonderful assortment of trees from all around the globe.

There are pleasant walks to be had along the harbour to Kastellet and Den Lille Havfrue (the Little Mermaid), and around Christiania, where you will come across some of the craziest-shaped houses you could ever imagine. Another popular spot to relax is around the Three Lakes. If you want to soak up the atmosphere of Nyhavn, with its expensive canal-side cafés, grab a beer from the supermarket and sit by the canal.

If you are lucky you will find some of the city's free bicycles (see pages 54–5) and you can cycle around the city for nothing but a 20kr returnable deposit.

Sitting on Hans Christian Andersen's lap in Rådhuspladsen for a photo is silly, but everyone does it. And wandering into the lobby of the Radisson for a free seat in an egg chair while you admire the lampshades is worth the risk of being asked to leave.

◆ *Visit Thorvaldsens Museet on a Wednesday and get in for nothing*

When it rains

On a rainy day, go and get wet in Rådhuspladsen and look up at the Unibank building on the corner of H C Andersen Boulevard and Vesterbrogade. The whole corner of the building is a giant thermometer topped by a pair of moving statues. When it is sunny a girl on a bicycle moves into view while when it is raining her twin has an umbrella.

All the museums, art galleries, churches, department stores and castles will keep you busy for at least a week of rain. Ny Carlsberg Glyptotek (see pages 85–6) is particularly pleasant in the rain, as you can sit in the conservatory and pretend you are in the tropics. You could spend the whole day in Nationalmuseet (see pages 84–5) and never leave, eating lunch in the café and wandering around the history of the world. Go in without a floor plan and see how long it takes you to find your way out again.

The **Dansk Jødisk Museum** (Museum of Danish Jewish History ❸ Proviantpassagen 6 ❶ 33112218 Ⓦ www.jewmus.dk ❷ info@jewmus.dk) in the Royal Library Gardens is a worthy visit, while the **Tøjhusmuseet** (Royal Arsenal Museum ❸ Tøjhusgade 3 ❶ 33116037 Ⓦ www.thm.dk ❷ thm@thm.dk) in Slotsholmen is a collection of big and small guns through the ages.

The **House of Amber** (various locations ❸ Kongens Nytorv 2, Frederiksborggade 34, Langelinie Allé 36, Vesterbrogade 1b, Nygade 6 Ⓦ www.houseofamber.com) has, besides a large supply of amber jewellery and ornaments for you to buy, a museum of amber with chess sets, boxes, ornaments prehistoric creepy crawlies transfixed for all time.

In Vesterbrogade is **Københavns Bymuseum** (Copenhagen City Museum ❸ Vesterbrogade 59 ❶ 33210772 Ⓦ www.bymuseum.dk

🕐 10.00–16.00 Mon, Thur & Fri–Sun) with a history of the growth of the city and a collection of Søren Kierkegaard's possessions.

🔺 *You're in luck – the Unibank girl says it's going to be sunny*

On arrival

TIME DIFFERENCE

Copenhagen's clocks follow Central European Time (CET). During Daylight Saving Time (end Mar–end Oct), the clocks are put ahead by one hour.

ARRIVING

By air

Copenhagen Kastrup Airport (Ⓦ www.cph.dk) is 8 km (5 miles) southeast of the city. A modern and busy airport, there are 24-hour ATMs, exchange facilities (06.00–22.00), a small general store, post office, car-rental agencies and restaurants. The information desk (🕐 06.00–24.00) will dispense maps and the useful, free *Copenhagen This Week*. It can book hotels for a charge.

The airport is connected by rail to Copenhagen's Central Station. Trains leave approximately every ten minutes 05.00–24.00 and hourly 00.00–05.00. The 12-minute journey costs approximately 27kr. Ticket machines in the arrivals hall dispense tickets. You use the same tickets for the bus, train and metro.

Bus services (line 250S during the day and 96N at night) also connect the airport with Central Station. They run every 15 minutes and take about 25 minutes.

If you are staying in Nyhavn or around the Three Lakes take the metro to Kongens Nytorv and Nørreport.

Some low cost airlines use **Sturup Airport** (Ⓦ www.sturup.com) near Malmö in Sweden, just over the Øresund bridge. A Flybus connects with Ryanair arrivals, bringing passengers into Copenhagen in 55 minutes. A taxi from this airport to the train station in Malmö takes about 20 minutes and costs around 165–200kr.

By rail & road

International trains and coaches arrive in Copenhagen at Central Station (Hovedbanegården or København H). The station concourse has cafés, an internet café, foreign exchange, bike hire, left luggage, showers and an information centre (☎ 70131415 ⓦ www.dsb.dk 🕐 05.45–23.30).

By water

If you are arriving in Copenhagen by ferry the arrival point in the city is along the harbour north of Nyhavn (building works on the harbour are under way to bring the docking point closer into Nyhavn). A short walk or taxi will bring you to Kongens Nytorv, where you will find a metro stop and several buses.

IF YOU GET LOST, TRY …

Excuse me, do you speak English?
Undskyld, taler du engelsk?
Ornskewl, tala do ehng-ehlsg?

How do I get to …?
Hvordan kommer jeg til …?
Vohdan komma yai ti …?

Can you show me on my map?
Kunne du vise mig det på kortet?
Kooneh do veeseh mai di por korrdeht?

FINDING YOUR FEET

Copenhagen must be the easiest city in Europe to settle into.
The public transport is quick and efficient, everyone speaks better
English than you do and will gladly offer assistance and although
the currency is unfamiliar it is quickly learned. Many shops show
the equivalent price in euros, although few accept them.

The most difficult thing for British visitors will be remembering
that the traffic is on the other side of the road and that there are
cycle tracks along most roads, fairly distinguishable from pavements.
Crossing the street on a red man is breaking the law, so be careful
not to get a fine even if the street is empty of cars. You will notice too
that it is not the custom to hold doors open for the person behind
you; a couple of doors in the face will soon make that apparent.
Street crime, while not unknown, is certainly rarer than in other
European cities, but pickpocketers are on the increase.

ORIENTATION

Starting from your arrival point at Central Station, the city centre
stretches east, bounded along its southeast edge by the harbour.
To the east of Central Station across Rådhuspladsen is the long,
pedestrianised shopping street Strøget that runs parallel with
the harbour all the way to Kongens Nytorv, a second transport hub,
and to Nyhavn, where many of the hotels are situated. To the west
of Central Station is the other hotel-laden area of Vesterbro.

Travelling north from the Central Station brings you to the Three Lakes,
and beyond them is the trendy area of Nørrebro, full of shops and cafés.

Between Strøget and the harbour is a small island, Slotsholmen,
the financial and political heart of the city. South of there is
Christianshavn, with its curious community of Christiania.
Even further south is the island of Amager and the airport.

GETTING AROUND

Public transport

The metro system (☎ 70151615 ⓦ www.m.dk) has two lines, which connect the east and west of the city with the centre, but not with Central Station. Stations you are most likely to use are Nørreport, Kongens Nytorv and Christianshavn. The metro, like the bus service, is zoned and a basic ticket (just under 20Kr) carries you across two zones and can be transferred to a bus journey within those zones within the hour.

The S-train network radiates out from Central Station along nine routes, with two more on the ring. Destinations and times are shown in the station concourse and each stop is shown on the platform. On the newer trains, the complete route is displayed electronically so you can check where you are at any time. Buy a ticket and clip it yourself on the platform at the start of your journey. Inspectors travel on most trains and buses and failure to produce a clipped ticket results in an instant fine.

Buses are boarded at the front, where you pay the driver or clip your bus card, and exited in the middle. Useful bus routes are:

5A from Amager, past Slotsholmen and Rådhuspladsen to Nørrebro

6A from Frederiksberg to Østerbro via Central Station, Slotsholmen and Nyhavn

66 from Central Station to Christianshavn

1A from Østerbro to Amelienborg, Nyhavn, the city centre (National Museum, Slotsholmen), Central Station, Fisketorvet and the west

350S from Dragør to Amager, Christinshavn, Kongens Nytorv, Nørrebro and the northwest.

Single tickets can be bought at the start of each journey in the metro stations or on the bus. *Klippekort*, ten-clip tickets, offer slightly cheaper journeys. You can use the *klippekort* to transfer from the

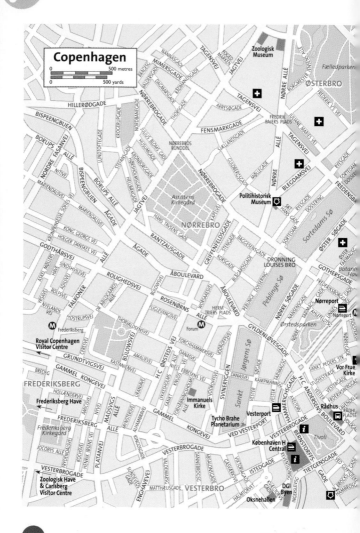

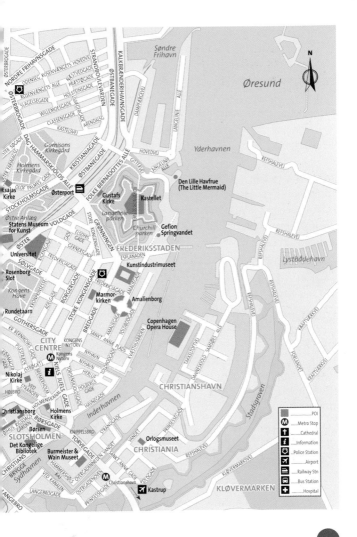

Søndre Frihavn

Øresund

Yderhavnen

Den Lille Havfrue
(The Little Mermaid)

Lystbådehavn

Gustafs Kirke

Kastellet

Gefion Springvandet

Churchill parken

FREDERIKSSTADEN

Kunstindustrimuseet

Marmor-kirken

Amalienborg

Copenhagen Opera House

CHRISTIANSHAVN

Inderhavnen

Stadsgraven

Holmens Kirke

Nikolaj Kirke

Christiansborg

Børsen

SLOTSHOLMEN

Det Kongelige Bibliotek

Burmeister & Wain Museet

Orlogsmuseet

CHRISTIANIA

KLØVERMARKEN

Kastrup

Esajas Kirke

Østerport

Statens Museum for Kunst

Universitet

Rosenborg Slot

Kongens Have

Rundetaarn

Kongens Nytorv

.......POI
Ⓜ ....Metro Stop
✝ ....Cathedral
ℹ ....Information
.......Police Station
✈ ....Airport
.......Railway Stn
.......Bus Station
✚ ....Hospital

53

metro to a bus within an hour and within the zones you have paid for. You can buy two-zone and three-zone *klippekort* tickets at railway stations and at vending machines along the bus routes. They must be stamped by you on the platform or bus.

Other offers include a 24-hour ticket, valid on all transport as far as Helsingør, and the **Copenhagen Card**, a discount card which gives you unlimited travel for 24 or 72 hours and reduced entrance to some sights.

Trishaws & cycling

Trishaws, tricycle rickshaws, can be hired around the town and make a green alternative to a conventional taxi. If you prefer to cycle yourself, between April and September the city operates a system of free bicycle use. At 125 stands around the city centre are racks where

a free bike can be removed by inserting a 20kr coin. The bikes have solid wheels with adverts on them and no gears. If your trip is in late August do not count on finding one. Bikes can also be rented from one of the many bike shops around the city for about 70kr a day.

Bicycles can be carried on S-trains in designated carriages and are easily parked. They may not be taken on the metro or bus. Some rules of the road should be noted however: bus passengers often alight onto the cycle path and cyclists must give way; cyclists may not turn left at major road junctions – they have to dismount and cross at the pedestrian crossing; stay on the right side of the cycle path; cyclists are allowed to overtake one another; when you decide to stop you should raise your right hand (do a 'how' sign) to signal to those behind you.

● *Try one of Copenhagen's eco-friendly taxis*

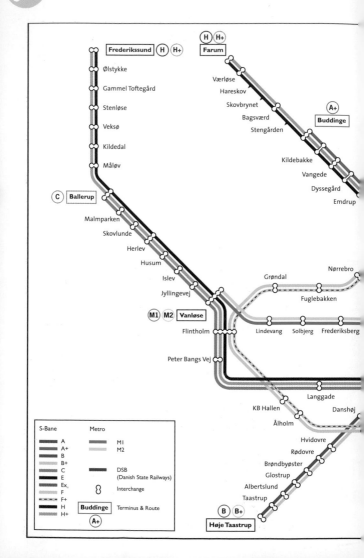

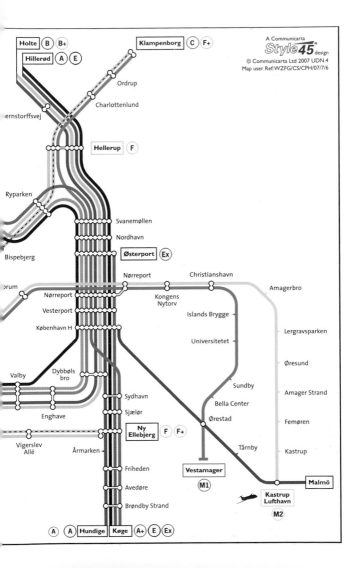

Driving

Getting around the city by car is manageable, although the city centre itself is best done on foot or by bicycle. Cars drive on the right. Car hire is easy and most hire companies do not require an international driving licence. To park you need a ticket, available from roadside machines, which you display inside the windscreen. The city is divided into zones with the more remote areas costing less to park in. If you are unsure of the zone and requirements, ask a local as a fine of over 500kr will be administered if you get it wrong.

CAR HIRE

The following companies have booths at the airport and an office in town:

Avis ⓐ Sluseholmen 3 ⓣ 33268080 ⓦ www.avis.dk
Budget ⓐ Vester Farimagsgade 7 ⓣ 33550500 ⓦ www.budget.dk
Europcar ⓐ Gammel Kongevej 13 ⓣ 33559900 ⓦ www.europcar.dk
Hertz ⓐ Vester Farimagsgade 1 ⓣ 33179010 ⓦ www.hertzdk.dk

● *Copenhagen's Nyhavn in spring*

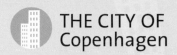

Nyhavn area

This is the epicentre of tourist Copenhagen. The broad pedestrianised shopping street called Strøget starts here with Kongens Nytorv (King's Square) at its head. To the east is Nyhavn (New Harbour), the short canal that once welcomed trading ships but which now houses a multitude of open-air restaurants, stylish hotels and swanky yachts. A short walk from here takes you to Amalienborg Slot (Amalienborg Palace), still lived in by the royal family but open to the public, where you can watch the changing of the guard. Further north along the harbour an old fortress, churches, gardens, museums, the photogenic Gefion Springvandet (Gefion Fountain) and the Little Mermaid – an overrated but essential stop on your itinerary – are all strung together along a harbourside walk with views over to the new opera house and Christianshavn.

SIGHTS & ATTRACTIONS

Amalienborg Slot (Amalienborg Palace)

The four palaces which make up Amalienborg, one of which is still lived in by the Queen of Denmark, were designed by the architect Nicolai Eigtved as homes for four of the city's wealthiest burghers but were commandeered by the royals after their own palace in Slotsholmen burned down. Architecturally tasteful rather than stunning, the courtyard buzzes with tourists snapping away. For a good laugh, don't miss the changing of the guard. A photogenic fountain fronts the courtyard but the real draw is Levetzau Palace, or Christian VIII's Palace, now a museum called The Royal Danish Collection, Amalienborg. It depicts the life and times of the Glücksburger dynasty, and is a storage facility for the Queen's library.

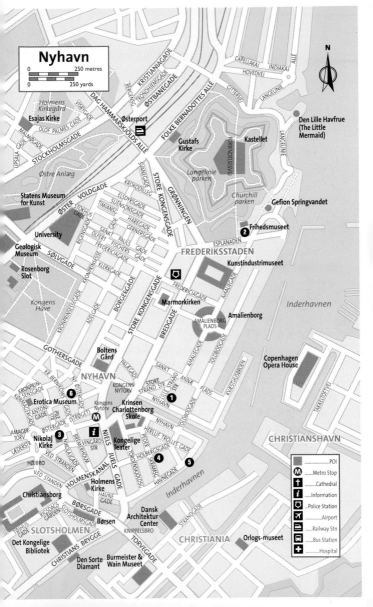

Nyhavn

| 0 | | | 250 metres |
| 0 | | | 250 yards |

N

Kristianiagade
Capellakaj   Indiakaj
Hovedvej
Dag Hammarskjølds Allé
Bergensg
Trondhjemsgade
Østbanegade
Folke Bernadottes Allé
Gitterveje
Langelinie
Langelinie Allé

Holmens Kirkegård

Vibygade

Esajas Kirke
Østport
Olof Palmes Gade

Gustafs Kirke
Kastellet
Den Lille Havfrue (The Little Mermaid)

Upsalagade
Malmøgade
Stockholmsgade

Langeliniparken
Forbindelsesvej
Langelinie

Østre Anlæg

Statens Museum for Kunst

Store Kongensgade
Grønningen
Churchill parken
Gefion Springvandet

Øster Voldgade
Krokodillegade
Elsdyrsgade
Suensonsgade
Timiangade
Haregade
Gernersgade

University
Storhus Gade
Rigensgade
Sankt Pauls Gade
Olfert Fischers Gade

Esplanaden
2 Frihedsmuseet

Geologisk Museum

Sølvgade
Fredericiagade
Klerkegade

FREDERIKSSTADEN

Rosenborg Slot

Kronprinsessegade
Borgergade
Adelgade

Kunstindustrimuseet

Kongens Have

Store Kongensgade
Bredgade
Fredericiagade

Inderhavnen

Marmorkirken
Amaliegade

Gothersgade

Boltens Gård

Store Kongensgade
Bredgade
Amalienborg Plads
Amalienborg
Toldbodgade

Palægade

NYHAVN

Kronprinsensgade
Kr. Bernikows Gade
Store Regnegade
Pistolstr
Antonigade
Østergade (Strøget)
Gothersgade
Ny Østergade

Erotica Museum **6**

Kongens Nytorv

Krinsen

Store Strandstr
Sankt Annæ Plads
Nyhavn
1
Kvæsthusbroen

Copenhagen Opera House

Takkelloftvej

Charlottenborg Skole

i
M
Niels Juels Gade
Vingårdsstr
Brolæggerstr
Nikolaj Gade
Ved Stranden

Kongelige Teater
Herluf Trolles Gade
Peder Skrams Gade
Nyhavn
Holbergsgade
Heibergsgade
Toldbodgade
4   **5**

CHRISTIANSHAVN

Amagertorv
Læderstr

Nikolaj Kirke **3**

Højbro
Ved Stranden

Holmens Kanal
Holmens Kirke
Havnegade
Hannegade

Inderhavnen

Christiansborg

Børsgade
Dansk Arkitektur Center

Tøjhusgade
Rigsdags Gården
Slotsholmsgade

Børsen
Knippelsbro

SLOTSHOLMEN

Strandgade

Det Kongelige Bibliotek

Christians Brygge

Den Sorte Diamant

Torvegade

Burmeister & Wain Museet

CHRISTIANIA

Orlogs-museet

	........POI
M	........Metro Stop
†	........Cathedral
i	........Information
C	........Police Station
✈	........Airport
	........Railway Stn
	........Bus Station
+	........Hospital

ⓐ Amalienborg Plads ☏ 33122188 ⓦ www.rosenborgslot.dk
🕒 10.00–16.00 May–Oct; 11.00–16.00 Tues–Sun, Jan–Apr & Nov–Dec.
Guided tours in English at 13.00 and 14.30 Sat & Sun 🚌 Bus: 1A, 6A,
15, 19; metro: Kongens Nytorv. Admission charge

Frederiksstaden

To the north of Nyhavn along the Langelinie waterfront promenade,
Frederiksstaden is a grand building project laid out by Frederik V
in the 18th century in celebration of the 300th anniversary of the
House of Oldenburg. Its wide boulevards and French-influenced
architecture were commissioned by various royal hangers-on to

🔻 *All roads lead to busy Kongens Nytorv*

designs by the architect Nicolai Eigtved. At its centre is Bredgade, full of classy boutiques and auction houses, and the pretty square of Sankt Annae Plads, with its church Garnisonskirken.

Gefion Springvandet (Gefion Fountain)

A walk along the harbour towards Langelinie on a sunny day is a treat in itself with the new opera house on the opposite bank, the tour boats chugging past and, best of all, no pedestrian crossings or cyclists. At its northern end is the Gefion Fountain. It was inaugurated in 1908, sponsored by Carlsberg and designed by Anders Bundegård. The fountain tells the story of the goddess Gefion, who, offered as much land as she could plough in a night, turned her sons into oxen

and created Danish Zealand. It is set in attractive parkland beside **St Alban's Church** (also known as the English Church), and creates some fascinating effects of light on water. ⓐ Amaliegade Ⓝ Bus: 1A, 15, 19, 26; S-train: Østerport

Kongens Nytorv (King's Square)

If you want to get your bearings in Copenhagen this is the place to start. Three main streets, Bredgade, Nyhavn and Strøget, radiate out from it and it forms a hub for journeys by metro and bus. The square itself, a huge cobbled garden with traffic roaring around it, comes alive in winter when an artificial ice rink is set up and during the summer often displays photographic and art exhibitions.

Around the square are some elegant buildings. **Det Kongelige Teater** (the Royal Theatre ⓐ Kongens Nytorv ⓣ 33696619 ⓦ www.kglteater.dk) was, before the opening of the new opera house, a major cultural centre, staging ballet, opera and dramatic performances in its two auditoria. It is now the city's centre for ballet after the construction of a new drama theatre along the harbour almost opposite the new opera house. The building is fairly recent, dating from 1872, but a theatre has been on this site since 1748. The statues which grace the exterior are some of the big names associated with the theatre's founding and it is worth wandering between the two buildings through the arch across Tordenskjoldsgade to admire the arch's ceiling frescoes.

Carrying on clockwise round the square brings you to Magasin du Nord, once the Hotel du Nord and now a classy department store known as Magasin. Hans Christian Andersen fans can wander up to the third floor, where the room he lived in for a time is open to the public.

⊙ *The Royal Guard at Amalienborg*

DEN LILLE HAVFRUE (THE LITTLE MERMAID)

One of the most frequently mutilated pieces of statuary in northern Europe, this diminutive creature has been beheaded on several occasions, lost limbs and suffered several other attacks of vandalism. It was commissioned in 1909 by beer magnate Carl Jacobsen (founder of Carlsberg) after watching an opera of the story by Hans Christian Andersen. More interesting is the daily circus around the statue, with hordes of tourists climbing out on to the rocks to have their photos taken and the tour boats lined up to pull in close for a better view. It's one of those things you just have to do. ❸ Langelinie Ⓝ Bus: 1A, 15, 19, 26; S-train: Østerport

Further clockwise again brings you to the 5-star Hotel d'Angleterre, another grand 18th-century building, where for not a small amount you can enjoy afternoon tea. The hotel always decorates its façade elaborately at Christmas time.

Marmorkirken (Marble Church)

A block west of the palace is this huge church aimed at rivalling St Peter's in Rome, begun in 1749 and due to financial problems completed only in 1894. The church is on an equally grand scale inside, although it is possible to make out the change in marble from expensive Norwegian to cheaper Danish which allowed the completion of the church. The real thrill of a visit to the church is not so much the interior as the trip to the top of the dome, which gives amazing views over the city. The journey upwards involves a tour guide, scrambling between the inner and outer roof domes and climbing through a trapdoor, but it is well worth the trip. Take note of the opening times and avoid wedding days, when the church is closed to the public. 🅐 Frederiksgade 4 🆃 33150144 🆆 www.marmorkirken.dk 🕒 10.00–17.00 Mon, Tue & Thur–Sat, 10.00–18.30 Weds, 12.00–17.00 Fri & Sun, Dome 13.00 & 15.00 Sat & Sun, 15 July–31 Aug 🚌 Bus 1A, 15, 19; metro: Kongens Nytorv. Admission charge for dome

Nyhavn (New Harbour)

Built in 1671 to bring ships into the centre of the city, the little canal has been gentrified in the last 30 years from a pretty sleazy docks area to a quaint, colourful, village-style place. The low-rise multicoloured buildings were once the homes and workplaces of merchants. In the 19th century three of these buildings (nos 20, 67 and 18) were home to Hans Christian Andersen, while the street itself became a red-light district. Today Nyhavn buzzes in summer with restaurants and the pavement is swathed in tables and chairs.

Upper Strøget

From Kongens Nytorv the long pedestrianised shopping street of Strøget begins at Østergade with all of the high-end fashion stores. This street will become familiar as your time in Copenhagen passes – it's difficult to walk down it without being drawn into its department stores, or sitting down to people-watch in one of its pavement cafés. Along here is the Guinness World of Records Museum, which always has a little cluster of people around it. There is always something to wonder at along this street, one of the longest pedestrianised streets in the world: those people dressed as statues or a string quartet or someone selling the latest piece of ephemera. Notice the change in the price and quality of the retail outlets as you head towards Rådhuspladsen.

CULTURE

Frihedsmuseet (Resistance Museum)

This purpose-built museum chronologically tells the story of the years of German occupation which Denmark suffered during World War II, their belated but increasing resistance to the occupation, the sacrifices of those brave enough to stand against Nazism, and their amazing decision in 1943 to ferry their Jewish population away to neutral Sweden in a succession of small boats in defiance of the Nazi orders for deportation to the death camps. In the grounds, open to the public in the summer months, is an underground shelter used during the war. Particularly poignant are the letters written to their families by resistance members who were executed for their efforts. ❷ Churchillparken 7 ☎ 33473921 Ⓦ www.frihedsmuseet.dk ⏰ 10.00–17.00 Tues–Sun, May–Sept; 10.00–15.00 Tues–Sun, Oct–Apr Ⓝ Bus: 1A, 15, 19, 26; S-train: Østerport

Kunstindustrimuseet (Museum of Decorative & Applied Art)

Housed in what was once the Frederiks Hospital, part of the great 18th-century development of Frederiksstaden, this collection, funded by the Carlsberg Foundation, contains over 300,000 items of furniture, ceramics, silver, textiles, carpets and more. A changing series of exhibitions is produced alongside the permanent collection. There is an excellent section of crafts from Asia, lots of Danish design – chairs especially – and the exhibitions are organised into time periods, so that you get a sense of the way design has changed over the centuries. The excellent café is furnished with lovely tables and chairs and the courtyard is an excellent place to rest tired feet after a good wander around. In the courtyard there is a plaque commemorating the life of the philosopher Kierkegaard, who died

⬥ *The dramatic Gefion Fountain*

in the hospital in 1855. ⓐ Bredgade 68 ⓣ 33185656
ⓦ www.kunstindustrimuseet.dk ⓛ 11.00–17.00 Tues–Sun
ⓜ Bus: 1A, 15, 19; S-train: Østerport; metro: Kongens Nytorv.
Admission charge, free Sun

Museum Erotica
Recent years have seen the cleaning up of the sex shops and
sleazy atmosphere of Vesterborg, so if you want to study sexually
permissive Denmark this might be the obvious place to go. Brightly

lit and about as erotic as a dental surgery, this is still a curious half hour's wander. Starting with ancient sex manuals and working its way through the history of punishments for prostitution, the museum arrives at recent times by way of some accounts of the sexual predilections of a few famous people. It pays homage to Marilyn Monroe in the form of one of her dresses and then sets about shocking visitors with porn movies. In the warm, almost comfy atmosphere of the museum the videos seem curiously sanitised. There is a shock room – darkly lit and containing photos of physical and sexual peculiarities. This is definitely not an 'oo-er missus' sort of place, but it is quite entertaining. ③ Købmagergade 24 ① 33120311 Ⓦ www.museumerotica.dk ◐ 10.00–23.00 May–Sept; 11.00–20.00 Sun–Thur, 10.00–22.00 Fri & Sat, Oct–Apr Ⓝ Bus: 5A, 6A, 350S; metro: Nørreport. Admission charge

RETAIL THERAPY

Here is the heart of shopping paradise. Visit the pedestrianised, café-lined street Strøget, its satellite streets Købmagergade, Kronprinsensgade and Læderstræde, and the smart stores around Kongens Nytorv. The two big department stores Illum and Magasin du Nord are handy.

Georg Jensen Everything you could ever want in silver. Worth going in just to admire the pieces. ③ Amagertorv 4 ① 33114080 Ⓦ www.georgjensen.dk ◐ 10.00–18.00 Mon–Thur, 10.00–19.00 Fri, 10.00–17.00 Sat

◗ *Amalienborg Palace, the royal winter residence*

Holmegaard Dedicated to glassware and crystal. ⓐ Amagertorv 8
ⓣ 33124477 ⓛ 10.00–18.00 Mon–Thur, 10.00–19.00 Fri, 10.00–17.00 Sat

Illums Bolighus A smaller department store selling beautiful
things for the house and home and a few items of clothing.
ⓐ Amagertorv 10 ⓣ 33141941 ⓛ 10.00–18.00 Mon–Thur, 10.00–19.00
Fri, 10.00–17.00 Sat

ParisTexas An attractive boutique with designer labels for men and
women. ⓐ Krystalgade 18–20 ⓣ 33363303 ⓛ 10.00–18.00 Mon–Thur,
10.00–19.00 Fri, 10.00–17.00 Sat

Royal Copenhagen Dedicated to the revered, over 200-year-old royal
porcelain. Has a small seconds store. ⓐ Amagertorv 6 ⓣ 33137181
ⓦ www.royalcopenhagen.com ⓛ 10.00–18.00 Mon–Thur,
10.00–19.00 Fri, 10.00–17.00 Sat

TAKING A BREAK

The obvious place for a coffee or lunch in the area is Nyhavn, where
in summer tables litter the waterside and you are spoilt for choice.
Back in Strøget the department stores have cool underground
coffee shops or you can sit out on the street and people-watch.

Hyttefadet £ ❶ A traditional Danish restaurant – perfect for
trying *smørrebrød*. Warm, welcoming, friendly service and
occasionally live music in the evenings. ⓐ Nyhavn 25 ⓣ 33120107
ⓦ www.hyttefadet.dk ⓛ 09.00–01.00 Sun–Thur, 09.00–02.00
Fri & Sat ⓝ Bus: 350S, 1A, 15,19; Metro: Kongens Nytorv

⬤ *Charming welcome from Sommerhuset café and restaurant*

Sommerhuset £–££ ❷ Garden café and restaurant set in a peaceful area by the Gefion Fountain. Danish specialities, a barbeque in the evenings and an extensive organic wine list. ❸ Churchillparken 7 ❶ 33321314 ⓦ www.cafesommerhuset.dk ◷ 09.00–24.00 May–Oct ⓝ Bus: 350S, 1A, 15,19, 26; S-train: Østerport

Caféen I Nikolaj ££ ❸ Housed in Nikolaj Kirke (Nikolaj Church), with charming indoor seating and a large terrace area. ❸ Nikolaj Plads 12 ❶ 33116313 ◷ 11.30–23.00 Mon–Sat, July, Aug & Dec; 11.30–17.00 Mon–Sat, Jan–June & Sept–Nov ⓝ Bus: 6A, 1A, 15,19, 26; Metro: Kongens Nytorv

AFTER DARK

Enjoy the early evening at any of the numerous bars in Nyhavn or in the streets between Upper Strøget and Købmagergade.

RESTAURANTS

Fuego ££ ❹ Argentinian restaurant and bar incorporating Spanish, German and Italian cuisine. Excellent wine list. Dancing on Thursdays. ⓐ Holbergsgade 14 ❶ 33131171 ❻ 18.00–24.00 Mon–Thur & Sun, 18.00–03.00 Fri & Sat ❶ Kitchen closes 22.00 during week and 21.30 on Sun ❷ Bus: 350S, 1A, 15,19; Metro: Kongens Nytorv

Custom House ££–£££ ❺ This beautiful old customs building has been transformed by Terrance Conran into three stylish, top calibre restaurants: Bacino (Italian), Bar&Grill (brasserie) and Ebisu (Japanese). There is even a deli. ⓐ Havnegade 44 ❶ 33310130 ⓦ www.customhouse.dk ⓔ info@customhouse.dk ❻ 09.00–22.00 Mon & Tue, 09.00–23.00 Wed–Sat, 11.00–22.00 Sun ❷ Bus: 350S, 1A, 15,19; Metro: Kongens Nytorv

L'Alsace £££ ❻ French restaurant, with foie gras and seafood a speciality. Pretty courtyard outdoor seating in summer. ⓐ Ny Østergade 9 ❶ 33145743 ⓦ www.alsace.dk ❻ 11.30–24.00 Mon–Sat ❷ Bus: 350S, 1A, 15, 19; Metro: Kongens Nytorv

CLUBS

Boltens Gaard Home to several of Copenhagen's clubs and bars. ⓐ behind Gothersgade 8 ❷ Bus: 350S, 1A, 15, 19; Metro: Kongens Nytorv

Emma One of Copenhagen's newer clubs, with a simple, chic interior and tasty cocktails. ⓐ Lille Kongensgade 16 ❶ 33112020 ⓦ www.emma.dk ⓔ info@emma.dk ❻ 23.00–05.00 Thur–Sat ❷ Bus: 350S, 1A, 15, 19; Metro: Kongens Nytorv

❶ *Enjoy a meal harbourside at Custom House*

Rådhuspladsen & the West

Rådhuspladsen, dominated at its southwestern corner by the grand Rådhus (Town Hall), is where the city's wheels turn. Early in the morning it bustles with people on their way to work, tables and chairs are drawn up into close huddles, and traffic roars across the huge road junctions that surround it. But later a sunny piazza emerges: coffee shops, hot dog stands, trinkets laid out on the ground, herds of tourists and shoppers heading for the southern end of Strøget, the long shopping street that leads to Kongens Nytorv. At night the surrounding buildings disappear to be replaced by disembodied blinking neon and the fairy lights of Tivoli.

Radiating out from the square is a fascinating series of contrasting tourist attractions, including Louis Tussaud's stands, the Dansk Design Centre, Tivoli, the Carlsberg Sculpture Centre, the grandiose Palace Hotel and Ripley's Believe It or Not Museum. Lording over it all is Copenhagen's most famous immigrant, Hans Christian Andersen, whose statue sits on the boulevard named after him.

SIGHTS & ATTRACTIONS

Carlsberg Brewery Visitor Centre

The Visitor Centre, in a brewing house built at the turn of the 20th century, displays the history of brewing and of the Carlsberg Brewery, which you can smell but not see. Unfortunately the free beer on your tour has been stopped, but you still have the opportunity to buy one. ❸ Gamle Carlsberg Vej 11 ❶ 33271314 ❽ www.visitcarlsberg.dk ❹ 10.00–16.00 Tues–Sun ❽ Bus: 6A, 18; S-train: Enghave. Admission charge

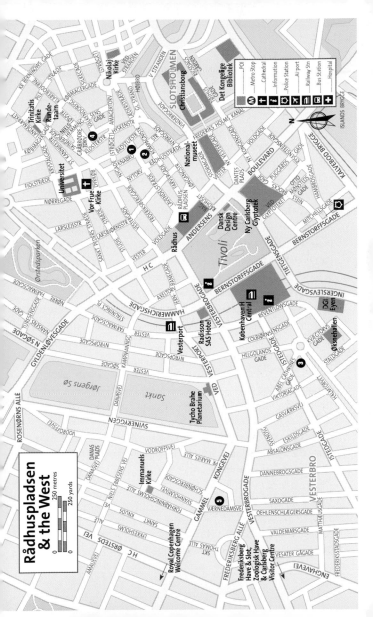

Rådhuspladsen & the West

0 ____ 250 metres
0 ____ 250 yards

Legend

M	POI
	Metro Stop
✝	Cathedral
i	Information
	Police Station
✈	Airport
R	Railway Stn
B	Bus Station
✚	Hospital

ROSENØRNS ALLÉ
VODROFFSVEJ
H C ØRSTEDS VEJ
AMALIEVEJ
THURESENSGADE
DANAS VEJ
DANAS PLADS
NIELS EBBESENS VEJ
SKT THOMAS ALLÉ
LYKKESHOLMS ALLÉ
SANKT KNUDS VEJ
FORHÅBNINGSHOLMS ALLÉ
SVANHOLMSVEJ
SCHØNBERGSGADE
FR MARIES ALLÉ
KONGEVEJ
VODROFFSVEJ
SVINERYGGEN

Immanuels Kirke

Royal Copenhagen Welcome Centre →

Frederiksberg Have & Slot, Zoologisk Have & Carlsberg Visitor Centre →

GAMMEL KONGEVEJ
VÆRNEDAMSVEJ
FREDERIKSBERG ALLÉ
VESTERBROGADE
SAXOGADE
OEHLENSCHLÆGERSGADE
VALDEMARSGADE
VESATER GÅGADE
ENGHAVEVEJ
FREDERIKSSTADSGADE
MATTHÆUSGADE
DANNEBROGSGADE

VESTERBRO

Tycho Brahe Planetarium

Sankt Jørgens Sø

VED
VESTER SØGADE
N SØGADE
GYLDENLØVESGADE
NANSENSGADE
TURESENSGADE
FARIMAGSGADE
NØRRE
ØRSTEDSPARKEN
FARIMAGSGADE
LARSLEJSSTR
NØRREGADE
FIOLSTRÆDE
KAMPMANNSG
NYROPSGADE
VESTER FÆLLEDVEJ
HAMMERICHSGADE
STALLINGS PL
AXELTORV
JERN BANEGADE
H C ANDERSENS
VESTERPORT
VESTER VOLDGADE
NØRREVOLDGADE

Vesterport

Radisson SAS Hotel

5

VIKTORIAGADE
ABEL CATHRINES
HELGOLANDS GADE
COLBJØRNSENSGADE
REVENTLOWSGADE
ISTEDGADE
GASVÆRKSVEJ
ESKILDSGADE
ABSALONSGADE
VIKTORIAGADE
V KIOSKVEJ
STALDGADE
ØKSNEHALLEN
Øksnehallen

3

DGI Eyen

DGI Byen

København H Central

i

VESTERBROGADE
BERNSTORFFSGADE
TIETGENSGADE
BERNSTORFFSGADE
INGERSLEVSGADE

i

Tivoli

Ny Carlsberg Glyptotek
Dansk Design Centre
Rådhus
Vor Frue Kirke

M

Universitet

✝

KLOSTERSTR
KRYSTALGADE
SKT PEDERS STRÆDE
SANKT PEDERS
VESTER VOLDGADE
STUDIESTRÆDE
LARSBJØRNSSTR
TEGLGÅRDSSTR
NØRRE VOLDGADE
VESTERGADE
FARVERGADE
LAVENDELSTRÆDE
GYLDENLØVESGADE
VANDKUNSTEN
KOMPAGNISTR
RÅDHUS PLADSEN
NYTORV
GAMMELTORV
NØRREGADE

4

Rundetaarn
Trinitatis Kirke

KØBMAGERGADE
SKINDERGADE
KRYSTALGADE
STORE KANNIKESTR
FIOLSTRÆDE
SVÆRTEGADE
SILKEGADE
GRØNNEGADE
VALKENDORFS G
GRÅBRØDRE TORV
KLAREBODERNE
NIELS HEMMINGSENS GADE
SKINDERGADE
AMAGERTORV
HØJBRO PLADS
ØSTERGADE
STRØGET
VIMMELSKAFTET
NYGADE
KLOSTERSTR
KØBMAGERGADE
LØVSTRÆDE
GAMMEL STRAND
NABOLØS
SNAREGADE
MAGSTRÆDE
KNABROSTRÆDE
HYSKENSTR
BADSTUESTR
NYBROGADE
RÅDHUSSTRÆDE
VINDEBROGADE
FREDERIKSHOLMS KANAL

1
2

National-museet

VED STRANDEN
GL STRAND
NYBROGADE

Nikolaj Kirke

SLOTSHOLMEN

Christiansborg

Det Kongelige Bibliotek

ISLANDS BRYGGE

KALVEBOD BRYGGE

FREDERIKSHOLMS KANAL
BØRSGADE
VINDEBROGADE
TØJHUSGADE
FREDERIKSHOLMS KANAL
NY KONGENSGADE
BREMERHOLM
HOLMENS KANAL
DANTES PLADS
VODGADE
STORMGADE
NYHAVN
PUGGÅRDSGADE
OTTO MØNSTEDS GADE
HAMBROGADE
MITCHELLSGADE
BERNSTORFFSGADE

N

Frederiksberg Have & Slot (Frederiksberg Park & Castle)

Huge, pleasant park littered with attractions. You could spend an afternoon out here visiting the sights, and the park makes a lovely break in between visits. On the south side is a museum of modern glass, the Cisterne. In the southeast corner is the Royal Danish Horticulture Garden, used in summer for outdoor concerts, while the Spa Room holds regular exhibitions and concerts. Beside the Horticulture Garden is the summer palace Frederiksberg Slot, which although not open to the public, is well worth admiring for its 18th-century Italianate style. There is also a zoo (see pages 83–4). Look out for the *Suttetræ* (dummy tree), on which growing children hang their old dummies as a farewell ritual. ● 07.00–17.00, 18.00 or 19.00 Oct–Mar; 07.00–21.00 or 22.00 Apr–Sept ⊙ Bus: 18, 6A

Cisterne Museet for Moderne Glaskunst ⓐ Søndermarken
ⓘ 33219310 ⓦ www.cisterne.dk ● 14.00–18.00 Thur & Fri, 11.00–17.00 Sat & Sun ⊙ Bus: 18, 6A. Admission charge

Lower Strøget

A series of linked pedestrianised streets – Nygade, Vimmelskafet, Amagertorv and Østergade – known collectively as Strøget. The streets here are littered with wares laid out on the ground, and string quartets or drum bands cheerfully busk on the pavement. At the junction with Nørregade are Gammeltorv and Nytorv (Old Square and New Square), with their centrepieces the Domhuset (Courthouse) and Caritas Fountain (1608).

● *Frederik VI welcomes you to Frederiksberg Have*

Rådhus (City Hall)

Rådhus was completed in 1905, the work of Danish architect Martin Nyrop. Look closely at the exterior and you will see a multitude of odd figures from gargoyle water spouts to fierce dragons guarding the entrance. You are free to wander about the equally ornate interior but a guided tour would make more sense of what you are seeing.

Take a look at the Jens Olsen's World Clock just inside the main entrance, with its 570,000-year calendar its multitude of shivering dials tell stunningly accurate time as well as plotting assorted planetary orbits and lunar and solar eclipses.

A tour of the bell tower involves 300 steps then a scramble to the spire, but there are some great views towards Kongens Nytorv. The building has a pretty enclosed garden which is good for a quiet break. 🄰 Rådhuspladsen 1 ❶ 33663366 🄻 07.45–17.00 Mon–Fri, 09.30–13.00 Sat, Guided tours in English 15.00 Mon–Fri, 10.00 & 11.00 Sat, minimum of four persons 🄽 Bus: 2A, 5A, 250S. Admission charge for clock, tower and tours

Radisson SAS Hotel

Designed by Arne Jacobsen in 1960. If you don't stay here you can lounge about the lobby or have a drink in the bar, if only to admire the crazy 1960s steel light fittings, swing about in the Jacobsen egg and swan chairs or admire the cute ashtrays. One of the rooms (606) has been preserved in its original style. In a case by the lifts are some of Jacobsen's designs, many of which you can buy over the road in the design shop. 🄰 Hammerichsgade 1 ❶ 33426000 🄦 www.radisson.com 🄽 Bus: 6A, 5A, 250S; S-train: København H

● *The lower end of Strøget offers plenty of free entertainment*

Royal Copenhagen Welcome Center

At the Royal Copenhagen porcelain factory you can watch the skilled artisans painting the world-famous tableware, or even try a painting course yourself. The factory outlet next door sells seconds at almost reasonable prices. ⓐ Søndre Fasanvej 5
ⓣ 38149297 ⓦ www.royalcopenhagen.com ⓛ 09.00–15.00 Mon–Fri, Factory shop 09.30–17.30 Mon–Fri, 09.00–14.00 Sat
ⓜ Metro: Frederiksberg. Admission charge

Tivoli

One of the oldest amusement parks in Europe, Tivoli is also one of Copenhagen's top tourist attractions. As darkness falls and the fairy lights hover over your head, the bandstands fill with music and the rides start to whirl. You will feel like you are ten years old again, just for a while. Save Tivoli for a warm night and enjoy a meal that will coincide with the nightly performances – programmes are posted up outside. Don't miss the sound and light show, on 30 minutes before the gardens close. Tivoli has its own fireworks factory and there are displays on Wednesdays and Saturdays at 23.45.

The daytime is for real children and gardeners. There are over 30 rides, pantomime performances, sticky things to eat and fairground stalls. Gardeners will admire the planting; someone with a real eye for design fills the beds. Beautiful weeping willows, linden and elm trees provide a backdrop to the nightly sound and light show and there isn't a municipal shrub to be seen. ⓐ Vesterbrogade 3
ⓣ 33151001 ⓦ www.tivoli.dk ⓛ 11.00–23.00 Sun–Thur & Fri 11.00–24.00 Sat, mid-Apr–mid-June & mid-Aug–mid-Sept;
11.00–24.00 Sun–Thur, 11.00–00.30 Fri & Sat, mid-June–mid-Aug;
11.00–22.00 Mon–Thur, 11.00–23.00 Fri & Sat, 11.00–21.00 Sun, late Nov–23 Dec. Closed Oct–late Nov, and late Dec–mid-Apr

Bus: 1A, 2A, 5A, 6A. Admission charge and charges for rides and some shows

Tycho Brahe Planetarium

IMAX theatre that uses state of the art technology to display the night skies, as well as showing stomach-churning movies. The planetarium is named after the great Danish astronomer Tycho Brahe (1546–1601) who discovered the constellation Cassiopeia (the Big Dipper). Gammel Kongevej 10 33121224 www.tycho.dk 9.30–21.00 Tues–Thur, 10.30–21.00 Fri–Mon S-train: Vesterport. Admission charge

Vesterbro

For a long time the part of the city which tourists first encounter – Central Station and many of the city's middle-range hotels are here, as was the red-light district – Vesterbro has become less obtrusive lately. There are still some sex shops, though, and a few junkies and alcoholics still congregate at the back of the station. As Vesterbrogade heads out west towards Frederiksberg the streets take on a decidedly more local atmosphere, with lots of small ethnic restaurants and take-aways from the Asian and Turkish immigrants who have settled in the area. Carry on further and as you near Frederiksberg Park you enter the net-curtained leafy suburbs where trendy designer boutiques and cafés, and fine-dining restaurants replace the fast-food outlets and cheap shops.

Zoologisk Have (Zoological Gardens)

Founded in 1859, this is one of Europe's oldest zoos. Although small by the standards of others, it provides comfortable accommodation for its captive animals. There is a children's section containing native farm animals, a section for animals from the South American pampas, others from the African savannah and an enclosure designed by Norman Foster for the zoo's three new elephants, a gift from the King of Thailand. Climb the 40 m (130 ft) tower for great views across the city. ❸ Roskildevej 32 ❶ 70200200 ❿ www.zoo.dk ❻ 09.00–18.00 June–Aug; 09.00–17.00 Mon–Fri, 09.00–18.00 Sat & Sun, Apr, May & Sept; 09.00–17.00 Oct; 09.00–16.00 Nov–Feb; 09.00–16.00 Mon–Fri, 09.00–18.00 Sat & Sun, Mar ❿ Bus: 6A, 4A. Admission charge

CULTURE

Nationalmuseet (National Museum)

Seeing everything in this museum in one day would be exhausting. A word of warning before you begin: get a plan of the exhibitions before you set out.

The Danish early history section comes mainly from Denmark's many bogs and fields – Viking helmets and *luren* (Bronze Age musical instruments), jewellery and weapons, a 1st-century chariot from Jutland, excavated Bronze Age graves, and the superb Trundholm Sun Chariot – a bronze model of the chariot of the sun god pulling the sun across the sky.

The upper floors continue the history of Denmark into medieval and Renaissance times with the largely ecclesiastical and royal exhibits, glistering with gold and jewels.

The ethnographic section is strong on Inuit culture, with sculptures, clothing, amulets and reams of whalebone, kayaks and harpoons. Other sections of the museum are dedicated to classical antiquities, including an exceptional collection of black- and red-figure Greek pottery.

DANSK DESIGN CENTER

This purpose-built showcase of Danish design holds a changing set of design exhibits, and the basement has a permanent collection of iconic items, such as wonderbras, tetrapaks, Jacobsen coffee pots and Dyson vacuum cleaners. An excellent shop sells collapsible travel gear. ⓐ H C Andersens Boulevard 27 ❶ 33693369 ⓦ www.ddc.dk ⓔ design@ddc.dk ⓛ 10.00–17.00 Mon, Tues, Thur & Fri, 10.00–21.00 Wed, 11.00–16.00 Sat & Sun ⓝ Bus: 2A, 5A, 6A, 250S. Admission charge

A children's museum packs all of these exhibits into a few experiences. Here you can play in the shop from Pakistan, pretend to sail in a Viking ship, fire crossbows and sit inside a Tuareg tent. A section dedicated to coins and an annexe called the Victorian Home (visit by guided tour only) plus a windmill from Christianshavn make up the rest of the collection. ⓐ Ny Vestergade 10 ❶ 33473850 ⓦ www.natmus.dk ⓛ 10.00–17.00 Tues–Sun ⓝ Bus: 1A, 2A, 5A. Admission charge, free Wed

Ny Carlsberg Glyptotek (Carlsberg Sculpture Centre)

This astonishing art collection, donated by beer baron Carl Jacobsen, needs at least a whole day to do it justice. If you can't spare that, you should decide if the French collection or the Mediterranean antiquities interest you most and focus on your art of choice.

The museum was built in 1897 around the beautiful Winter Garden, a conservatory filled with tropical plants and statues. The earlier collection donated by Jacobsen consists of hundreds of ancient artefacts tracing the history of sculpture from ancient Sumerian, through Egyptian, Phoenician to Greek, including a huge collection of Etruscan and ancient Greek items. The recently opened (1996) French wing has as its basis a collection of paintings by Paul Gauguin, who lived in Copenhagen for a few years, donated to the city by Jacobsen's son Helge. To this collection has been added works by Corot, Renoir, Monet, Pisarro, Cézanne, Toulouse-Lautrec and Van Gogh. Danish art is well represented here too. The Winter Garden has an excellent café where you can eat your Danish among the palm trees to the sound of the Water Mother with Children fountain. ⓐ Dantes Plads 7 ❶ 33418141 ⓦ www.glyptoteket.dk ⓔ info@glyptoteket.dk ⓛ 10.00–16.00 Tues–Sun ⓝ Bus: 2A, 5A, 6A. Admission charge, free Sun

Øksnehallen

This beautiful building was originally where oxen and cows stood in line before being sent to the slaughter house. It is now a huge exhibition and culture centre hosting many of Copenhagen's major events. All the buildings surrounding the hall have also maintained their original exterior and now house a variety of art houses, youth centres and laid-back cafés playing live music at the weekends. In contrast to these old dark brick buildings, just in front is the revamped Halmtorvet, which is a real hotspot in the summer for Copenhageners to hang out on the forecourts of trendy cafés and restaurants. ⓐ Halmtorvet 11 ❶ 33860400 ⓦ www.oeksnehallen.dk ⓛ 11.00–18.00 depending on the exhibition ⓝ Bus: 1A; S-train: København H

RETAIL THERAPY

Birna Fashion concept store created by an Icelandic designer. Good design, quality, practicality and individuality. ⓐ Istedgade 99 ⓘ 33257913 ⓦ www.birna.net ⓔ conceptshop-dk@birna.net ⓛ 11.00–18.00 Mon–Thur, 11.00–19.00 Fri, 11.00–16.00 Sat

Designer Zoo Several glass designers working on the premises make the pieces as you watch. Worth the trek. ⓐ Vesterbrogade 137 ⓘ 33249493 ⓦ www.dzoo.dk ⓛ 10.00–17.30 Mon–Thur, 10.00–19.00 Fri, 10.00–15.00 Sat

The Latin Quarter Sandwiched between Nørre Voldgade and Lower Strøget is the trendy Latin Quarter, which is littered with alternative shops selling men's and women's fashion, accessories and music. There are also several good second hand stores – look out for **København K (KBHK)** ⓐ Larsbjørnstræde 9 & Studiestræde 32b ⓘ 33330889 ⓛ 11.00–18.00 Mon–Thur, 11.00–19.00 Fri, 11.00–15.00 Sat, closed Sun ⓝ Bus: 5A, 6A, all routes to Rådhuspladsen

POD Clever home accessories to amuse your friends or fill stockings. ⓐ Sankt Peders Stræde 22 ⓘ 33161766 ⓛ 11.00–18. 00 Mon–Fri, 11.00–15.00 Sat

Saint Tropez One of Denmark's leading designer chain stores with locations in Germany, Sweden and Ireland, selling Saint Tropez fashion designs for women. Lower prices than boutique designers, but good quality clothing and accessories. ⓐ Vesterbrogade 41 ⓘ 33310017 ⓦ www.sainttropez.com ⓛ 10.00–18.00 Mon–Thur, 10.00–19.00 Fri, 10.00–16.00 Sat, closed Sun ⓝ Bus: 6A

TAKING A BREAK

Wander down Kompagnistræde, which runs parallel to Strøget between Rådhuspladsen and Illum and which has numerous cafés and restaurants. On the opposite side lies Gråbrødre Torv, a quaint 18th-century square circled with cafés and restaurants. Towards Veserbro, there is no shortage of options at Halmtorvet, the side streets off of Vesterbrogade and along Istedgade.

Café Sorgenfri £ ❶ 'No Worries Café'. Traditional Danish lunch in museum-like surroundings. ⓐ Brolæggerstræde 8 ❶ 33115880 ⓦ www.cafesorgenfri.dk ⓛ 11.00–23.00 Mon–Sat, 12.00–22.00 Sun ⓝ Bus: 5A, 6A

Rizraz £ ❷ Vegetarian all-day buffet with a Mediterranean twist, and lots for carnivores too. Great value. ⓐ Kompagnistræde 20 ❶ 33150575 ⓦ www.rizraz.dk ⓛ 11.30–24.00 ⓝ Bus: 5A, 6A

AFTER DARK

RESTAURANTS

Apropos ££ ❸ During the day a smart café bar serving lunches to city workers, at night this place has a classier menu, an excellent wine list and modern fusion dishes. Vegetarian menu also. ⓐ Halmtorvet 12 ❶ 33231221 ⓦ www.cafeapropos.dk ⓛ 10.00–24.00 Sun–Thur, 10.00–01.00 Fri & Sat ⓝ Bus: 2A, 5A, 66, 250S; S-train: København H

Bøf & Ost ££ ❹ Beautiful 18th-century building, and the best reputation in Copenhagen for a good *bøf* (steak). Also serves

great fish and a wide selection of *ost* (cheese). ⓐ Gråbrødretorv 13
ⓣ 33119911 ⓦ www.boef-ost.dk ⓔ reservation@boef-ost.dk
ⓛ 11.30–01.00, Kitchen 11.30–22.30 ⓝ Bus: 5A, 6A, 14; S-train: Nørreport

Les Trois Cochons ££ ❺ Brasserie and bar, limited menu but
fantastic food in the unique location of an old butchery. Look out
for its sister restaurants Auberge and Cofoco, and the Le Marché
deli and take-away. ⓐ Værnedamsvej 10 ⓣ 33317055 ⓦ www.cofoco.dk
ⓛ 13.00–22.00 Mon–Sat, 16.00–22.00 Sun ⓝ Bus: 6A;
S-train: Vesterport

CLUBS
Cirkusbygninen (The Circus Building) Hosts the Wallmans Dinnershow.
Multi-level seating, several bars and a good view of the performance.
Keep an eye out for what is on. ⓐ Jernbanegade 8 ⓣ 33163700
ⓦ www.wallmans.dk ⓝ Bus: 5A, 6A, 66; S-train: Vesterport
or København H

Copenhagen Jazz House The leading jazz club in the city. Live music
three nights a week and Nat Clubben, the nightclub, at weekends.
ⓐ Niels Hemmingssengade 10 ⓣ 33152600 ⓦ www.jazzhouse.dk
ⓛ 18.00–24. 00 Sun–Thur, 18.00–05.00 Fri & Sat. Admission charge
ⓝ Bus: 5A, 6A, 14; S-train: Nørreport

Mojo Live blues nightly. ⓐ Løngangstræde 21c ⓣ 33116453
ⓦ www.mojo.dk ⓛ 20.00–05.00. Admission charge ⓝ Bus: 5A, 6A

Pumphuset Live music every weekend by prominent artists in an
intimate venue. ⓐ Studiestræde 52 ⓣ 33931960 ⓝ Bus: 5A, 6A, 250S;
S-train: København H or Vesterport

Christianshavn & Slotsholmen

The two neighbouring islands of Slotsholmen and Christianshavn couldn't be more different. Slotsholmen is the political and financial heartland of the country. The Parliament meets here, and it was the home of the royal family until the palace burned down. Every inch of this tiny island, where the city of Copenhagen had its origins, is covered with landmark buildings.

Christianshavn, the area of Christiania especially, is a very different kettle of fish. Christiania has, for many years, existed outside of the laws of the city. Its citizens, a motley combination of alternative types and sensible law-abiding citizens, paid no rates or rents and until a few years ago, and you could buy cannabis at your leisure from the stalls along so-called Pusher Street. The rest of the island, Christianshavn, is rapidly becoming a very bijou area with some of the city's most exclusive restaurants housed in the renovated warehouses along the canal side.

SIGHTS & ATTRACTIONS

Bibliotekshaven (Royal Library Gardens)

This tranquil little garden is hidden down an alley off Rigsdagsgården. Almost perfect in design, it has a central pond, fountain and some very complacent ducks, pretty lawns and beautiful flower borders. Even Kierkegaard, usually a solemn figure, looks pleased to be here.
ⓐ Rigsdagsgården ⓑ 06.00–22.00 ⓝ Bus: 1A, 2A, 15, 26, 29, 66

Børsen (Stock Exchange)

Europe's oldest stock exchange, built between 1619 and 1640 by Christian IV, who had grand plans for Copenhagen as the financial

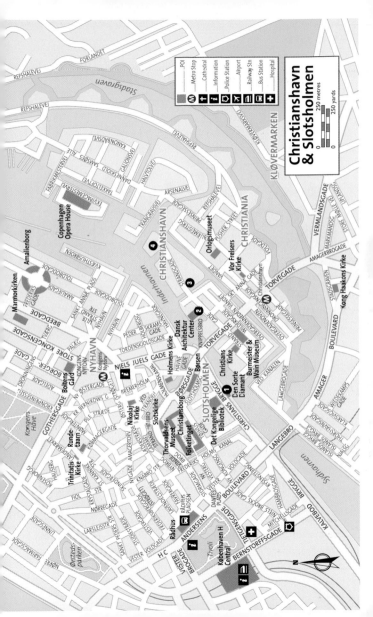

Christianshavn & Slotsholmen

■	POI
Ⓜ	Metro Stop
✚	Cathedral
ⓘ	Information
✈	Airport
🚆	Railway Stn
🚌	Bus Station
✚	Hospital

0 — 250 metres
0 — 250 yards

REFSHALEVEJ

FORLANDET

REFSHALEVEJ

Stadsgraven

KLØVERMARKEN

KRUDTLØBSVEJ

Copenhagen Opera House

Amalienborg

Marmorkirken

CHRISTIANSHAVN

CHRISTIANIA

Orlogsmuseet ④

Vor Frelsers Kirke

PUSHER STREET

③

TORVEGADE

Kong Haakons Kirke

Dansk Arkitektur Center ②

Børsen

Christians Kirke

Burmeister & Wain Museum

Den Sorte Diamant ①

SLOTSHOLMEN

Det Kongelige Bibliotek

Holmens Kirke

NIELS JUELS GADE

Nikolaj Kirke

Slotskirke

Thorvaldsens Museet

Folketinget

NYHAVN

Boltens Gård

Kongens Nytorv

Rundetaarn

Trinitatis Kirke

Christiansborg

Rådhus

Tivoli

København H Central

AMAGER

LANGEBRO

Sydhavnen

KALVEBO BRYGGE

Østedsparken

Kongens Have

● *Børsen, the old stock exchange*

capital of Europe. Now the Chamber of Commerce, it is not open to the public, but you can stand outside and marvel at the fantasy architecture – a 54 m (177 ft) copper spire in the form of intertwining dragons' tails bearing three golden crowns at their ends, representing the three golden nations of Denmark, Sweden and Norway. The stonework is a riot of embellishments and excesses. ● Børsgade ● Bus: 1A, 2A

Christiania

Just across the canal from Slotsholmen but far, far away culturally and economically, is Christiania. It is full of Peter Pans who flew away in the 1970s and never went home, artists, alcoholics, and now tourists after the thrill of wandering around a genuinely alternative society. To see some quirky designer houses, go for a stroll around the lakes at the back.

Pusher Street, previously a drug haven, has been cleaned up, and quartets of Danish policemen, probably the only ones you will see on your trip to Copenhagen, wander around the place making sure that the stalls laden with hash don't reappear. The cafés, graffiti and wild pot plants still remain.

There are some excellent craft, clothes and antique shops, several good restaurants and live music venues, stalls selling bongs and pipes, ethnic clothes, and right at the entrance a good café and information centre. The most popular souvenir is the Free Christiania t-shirt. Note that there are no ATM machines in Christiania and no-one accepts credit cards. You should also refrain from taking photographs. 🅐 Princessgade 🅣 32956507 🅦 www.christiania.org 🅛 Guided tours 15.00 26 June–31 Aug, Information centre 12.00–18.00 Mon–Thur, 12.00–16.00 Fri 🅝 Bus: 66; metro: Christianshavn

Christiansborg Slot (Christiansborg Castle)

Vast labyrinth of buildings, a maze if you don't know what to look for. The Danish tendency to make signs unobtrusive has been taken to a fine art here and it is possible to wander right through the place without noticing any of the doors you need to call in at.

A castle of some sort has stood here since 1147 although the present edifice dates back only to the early 20th century. The best approach to the palace is over the Marble Bridge across Frederiksholm Canal and into the outer courtyard of the palace. Over to your left across a parade ground an unadorned and bolted door is the entrance to the Royal Reception Rooms, the only bit of the royal family's part of the palace that you can visit. It is still used by the Queen and visited by guided tour (in cloth slippers) only.

Grandiose halls are lined with elaborate inlaid marble, and there is beautiful hand-painted wood panelling and a series of brilliantly coloured tapestries by Bjørn Nørgaard telling the story of Denmark. Also in here is the fascinating portrait of the royal family which includes several heads of European states and which you will see reproduced in several of the other royal palaces. The palace houses the Parliament, the Supreme Court and the Prime Minister's office. ⓐ Slotsholmen ⓣ 33926494 ⓦ www.ses.dk ⓛ Guided tours in English 11.00, 13.00 & 15.00 May–Sept; 15.00 Tues–Sun, Oct–Apr ⓝ Bus: 1A, 2A, 15, 26, 29. Admission charge

Christiansborg Slotskirke (Palace Chapel)

Copenhagen has a history of fires and this church, built in 1826, is no exception. After surviving a major fire in 1884 that destroyed the palace, this church was nearly devastated during restoration work in the early 1990s, when a firework set the scaffolding alight and destroyed the roof. Designed by the architect C F Hansen, its neoclassical marble interior, beautiful ceiling friezes by Thorvaldsen and reliefs by Karen Blixen are a treat. It is a quiet place to retreat from the traffic whirling around Slotsplads. Services are no longer held here.

🅐 Christiansborg Slotsplads 🕿 33926451 🕸 www.ses.dk 🕒 12.00–16.00 Sun, Aug–June; 12.00–16.00 July–Oct 🚌 Bus: 1A, 2A, 15, 26, 29

⬤ *Christiania is a great place for connoisseurs of outdoor art*

Folketinget (Danish Parliament)

Out from the arch between the two wings of the palace brings
you into Christiansborg Slotsplads, the main square in front of
the Parliament building where most political protests are held.
Round the side is the unmarked entrance to the Parliament.
You can wander up to the public gallery while the 179 Parliament
members are sitting or take the tour in English. This lets you
see the enormous *Vandrehal* (Hall of Wanderers), where the
Danish Constitution is kept. ❷ Rigsdagsgården ❶ 33375500
Ⓦ www.folketinget.dk ❻ During parliamentary session & for
guided tours 14.00 Mon–Sun, July–Sept; 14.00 Sun, Oct–June
❷ Bus: 1A, 2A, 15, 26, 29

Gammel Strand

Across the bridge by the Slotskirke is a laid-back, canal-side street,
great for a coffee and Danish while you rest from sightseeing.
The strand has an ancient history: in medieval times fishermen
landed their catch here and fresh fish was sold along this road
by fishwives, one of whom is commemorated in the statue by the
bridge. Lots of the cafés here still base their cuisine on fish. At no. 48
is Kunstforegningen, an exhibition space for good photography.

Holmens Kirke (Navy Church)

The Church of the Royal Navy stands just across the canal from
Børsen and was originally built in 1562 as a naval forge. Around the
time that construction of Børsen began the building was converted
into a church for the navy and the present structure came into
being in 1649. The austere Lutheran exterior gives way inside to
a highly ornate pulpit and carved oak altarpiece. Several important
figures from Danish naval history are interred in the burial chapel

and the present Queen took her marriage vows here. ❹ Holmens Kanal 9 ❶ 33136178 ❿ www.holmenskirke.dk ❻ 09.00–14.00 Mon–Fri, 09.00–12.00 Sat, Services on Sun ❷ Bus: 1A, 15, 26, 29

De Kongelige Stalde & Kareter (Royal Stables & Coaches)

The outer courtyard of the palace is still used as a working training ground and exercise yard for the royal horses, used on state occasions for the royal carriages. The stables themselves survived the fire in 1794 and once housed 200 animals. In those days even royal horses lived lavish lifestyles, as can be seen from the marble columns and vaulted ceilings. The royal carriages and an ancient Bentley also have a home here. ❹ Christiansborg Ridebane ❶ 33402676 ❿ www.ses.dk ❺ staldmesteren@kongehuset.dk ❻ Call for opening hours ❷ Bus: 1A, 2A, 15, 26, 29

Ruinerne Under Christiansborg (Christiansborg Ruins)

Hidden away inside the arch which joins the royal and governmental sections of Christiansborg Palace are the excavated foundations of several earlier buildings, including those of the city's original fortress (see page 14).

In a clearly different style are the remains of the *Blå Tårn* (Blue Tower), Denmark's one-time major prison. Princess Eleonore Christine, daughter of Christian IV, was held here for allegedly being involved in a plot against her father. The ruins are laid out in the centre of a circular walkway with spotlights highlighting identifiable parts of the older buildings. Rooms off the central area display artefacts discovered during the excavations. Captions are in English and work well to clarify what you are actually looking at, and the dim light and sounds of dripping water add an air of mystery. ❹ Christiansborg Slot ❶ 33926492 ❿ www.ses.dk ❻ 10.00–16.00

DEN SORTE DIAMANT (THE BLACK DIAMOND)

In contrast to the 17th-century Royal Library, with its red brick and Boston ivy homeliness, is the startling modernity of this black granite and glass extension. Up close there is a definite sense of vertigo as the building sheers off towards the water's edge, reflections of the surrounding buildings on the smooth black surface adding to the sense of confusion. Inside, across sandstone floors, the escalator brings you to a huge library of books and a walkway to the old library. In the basement is the National Photography Museum, which has a changing series of exhibits. Outside the building, students lounge about in café deckchairs, drinking coffee and soaking up the sun. There is also a fine dining restaurant called Søren K (🕐 12.00–24.00 Mon–Sat), a less formal café Øjeblikket (🕐 09.00–19.00 Mon–Sat) and a good bookshop. ❸ Søren Kierkegaard Plads 1 ❶ 33474747 ⓦ www.kb.dk 🕐 Library open 10.00–19.00 Mon–Fri, 10.00–14.00 Sat ⓧ Bus: 66

May–Sept; 10.00–16.00 Tues–Sun, Oct–Apr ⓧ Bus: 1A, 2A, 15, 26, 29. Admission charge

Vor Frelsers Kirke (Church of Our Saviour)

En route to Christiania along Sankt Annægade you'll pass this 1696 church with its baroque altar and a huge organ resting on the backs of two stucco elephants. The real reason to visit is the trip up the 400 steps to the top of the spire, the last 150 of them being on the outside of the building. Not a journey for those of a nervous disposition, but if you can brace yourself against the vertigo there are some stunning views from the top. King Christian was the first to make the climb, in 1752 when the tower was inaugurated. If you are here when there is a church service it is worth hanging about to hear the organ being played. ⓐ Sankt Annægade 29 ⓣ 32572998 ⓦ www.vorfrelserskirke.dk ⓛ 11.00–16.30 Mon–Sat, 12.00–16.00 Sun Apr–Aug; 11.00–15.30 Mon–Sat, 12.00–15.30 Sun, Sept–Mar, Tower closed Nov–Mar ⓝ Bus: 66; metro: Christianshavn. Admission charge for the tower

CULTURE

The Copenhagen Opera House

Donated by the A P Møller and Chastine McKinney Møller foundation (founders of the shipping company Mærsk), the opera house is entirely the work of Danish artists and designers. The imposing exterior, designed by architect Henning Larsen, is controversial but impressive. Located in Holmen, across the harbour from Amalienborg, nothing is cheap in this building. You can take guided tours (recommended), eat in the restaurant or watch a performance, but be prepared to part with at least 100kr. ⓐ Ekvipagemestervej 10 ⓣ 33696933 ⓦ www.operaen.dk ⓔ admin@kglteater.dk ⓛ Guided tours 09.30 & 16.30 Sat & Sun ⓝ Bus: 66

Orlogsmuseet (Royal Danish Naval Museum)

Set in a former naval hospital in Christianshavn, the museum houses over 300 model boats built from the 16th to the 19th century. Many were working models made by the men who built the real thing, to show to their sponsors, and range from cutaway models to fully rigged, seagoing but tiny ships. There are also carved wooden figureheads, beautiful brass instruments and a replica submarine,

plus a café. ⓐ Overgaden Oven Vandet 58 ❶ 33116037
ⓦ www.orlogsmuseet.dk 🕐 12.00–16.00 Tues–Sun
Ⓝ Bus: 2A, 66. Admission charge

Thorvaldsens Museet

Museum focusing on the sculptures of Bertel Thorvaldsen
(1768–1844), one of Denmark's most famous sons. As a sculptor
he made his name in Rome while learning his craft and was heavily
influenced by Greek and Roman statuary. His return to Copenhagen
towards the end of his life brought about an artistic revival in the
city. His output bordered on the manic and this museum, purpose-
built at the expense of the royal family, houses masses of his work.
The ground floor consists largely of monumentally huge but very
dusty plaster casts which were used in the creation of his great
works of statuary, set along long corridors beautifully lit by natural
light. The upper storey of the building contains his personal art
collection. In the corridors you will meet Byron, Walter Scott, Christ
and figures from Greek and Roman mythology. Be sure to look
up at the ceilings in each room, as they are all unique. ⓐ Bertel
Thorvaldsens Plads 2 ❶ 33321532 ⓦ www.thorvaldsensmuseum.dk
🕐 10.00–17.00 Tues–Sun Ⓝ Bus: 1A, 2A, 15, 26, 29. Admission charge,
free Wed and for children

RETAIL THERAPY

Carl Madsens Plads Open-air market in Christiania where you can
buy politically oriented t-shirts, ethnic woollens, skunk seed, bongs
and the like.

Christiania Bikes Fun to browse, even if you won't fit one of their bikes on the plane. ⓐ Refshalevej 2 ⓣ 32548748 ⓦ www.christianiabikes.dk ⓛ 09.00–17.00 Mon–Fri, 10.00–14.00 Sat ⓝ Bus: 2A, 66, 350S

Dansk Arkitektur Center Book Shop Housed in the old dock area, the Nordic region's largest collection of Danish and international design and architecture books. ⓐ Strandgade 27b ⓣ 32571930 ⓦ www.dac.dk ⓛ 10.00–17.00 Mon–Fri ⓝ Bus: 2A, 66, 350S

Gammel Strand Flea Market Flea market open from spring to autumn, with good antiques. ⓛ 09.00–18.00 Fri, 09.00–15.00 Sat ⓝ Bus: 1A, 2A, 6A

Ginnungagab Leather, fur and woollen items from the Nordic countries and Greenland. Also sells organic snacks. ⓐ Overgaden oven Vandet 4a ⓣ 32542211 ⓛ 11.00–18.00 Tues–Fri, 11.00–15.00 Sat

Kvindesmedjen The women's blacksmith shop makes all sorts of handicrafts out of metal. ⓐ Mælkevejen 83e ⓣ 32577658 ⓦ www.kvindesmedien.dk ⓛ 09.00–17.00 Mon–Fri, 11.00–15.00 Sat

TAKING A BREAK

There are several outdoor cafés in Christiania, but it is not a particularly restful place. Head out past Vor Frelsers Kirke toward the canals and you'll find several canal-side bars and cafés along Sankt Annæ Gade. In Slotsholmen the place to relax is Øieblikket, in the lobby of the new library, or pop over to Gammel Strand, great for coffee, beer, lunch or just people-watching.

Øieblikket £ ❶ Good cakes and sandwiches; deckchairs in summer looking out over the waterfront. ⓐ Søren Kierkegaards Plads 1 ⓛ 09.00–19.00 Mon–Sat ⓝ Bus: 66

Dansk Arkitektur Center Café £–££ ❷ Book a window table for lunch for the best view over the harbour. Fresh, well-prepared food. ⓐ Strandgade 27b ⓣ 32578930 ⓛ 11.00–16.00 ⓝ Bus: 2A, 66, 350S

▲ *Kanalen offers high-class cuisine in a romantic setting*

AFTER DARK

Christianshavn has one or two excellent restaurants worth seeking out if you want to splash out on a really nice meal. For late-night larks find your way to Christiania.

RESTAURANTS

Restaurant Kanalen £££ ❸ High-class restaurant on the canal. Busy and traditionally Danish at lunch, but candle-lit, romantic and French-inspired cuisine at night. ⓐ Wilders Plads 2 ❶ 32951338 Ⓦ www.restaurant-kanalen.dk Ⓛ 11.30–24.00 Mon–Sat, Kitchen 11.30–15.00 & 17.30–22.00 ⓝ Bus: 2A, 66, 350S

Noma £££+ ❹ Style, substance and 2 Michelin stars are the draws at this converted 18th-century warehouse, where local ingredients and methods of cooking have been used to make a very original menu. ⓐ Strandgade 93 ❶ 32963297 Ⓦ www.noma.dk Ⓔ noma@noma.dk Ⓛ 18.00–01.00 Mon–Sat (kitchen closes 22.00) ⓝ Bus: 2A, 66, 350S

CLUBS

Loppen Laid-back club and performance venue in the heart of Christiania. Big names as well as smaller bands. ⓐ Christiania Sydområdet 4b ❶ 32578422 Ⓛ 21.00–late Mon–Thur ⓝ Bus: 2A, 66, 350S

Around the Three Lakes

Three constructed lakes, Sortedams Sø, Peblinge Sø and Sankt Jorgens Sø, mark the northern boundary of the city centre. To the north lie the suburbs of Nørrebro, Copenhagen's bohemian quarter, and Østerbro, with its stadium and park. To the south are the Botanical Gardens, Rosenberg Slot and Statens Museum for Kunst (the Danish National Gallery). Around the lakes themselves are some of Copenhagen's most exclusive apartment blocks, and a network of paths. On summer afternoons they come alive with Copenhageners jogging, strolling and meeting up with friends and family.

SIGHTS & ATTRACTIONS

Blågårdsgade
Slightly more bohemian than Sankt Hans Torv is this pedestrianised street off Nørrebrogade, full of interesting cafés and with a multicultural feel. Immigrant communities have settled in the area, establishing inexpensive ethnic restaurants and grocery stores. Blågårds Plads, with its many restaurants and cafés, turns into an ice skating rink in winter. ⓝ Bus: 5A, 350S

Botanisk Have & Museum (Botanical Gardens)
Built in 1874, the 10 hectare (25 acre) Botanical Gardens were originally part of the city's defensive ramparts. The moat and walls are now a garden pond and rockery. The garden is filled year round with excellent planting, which offers pretty bowers, shaded walks, a well laid-out tropical and subtropical glasshouse and an orchid house. Also within the grounds are the park's little museum, Botanisk Museum, which has exhibitions of botanical interest. ⓐ Øster Farimagsgade 2b ⓣ 35322222

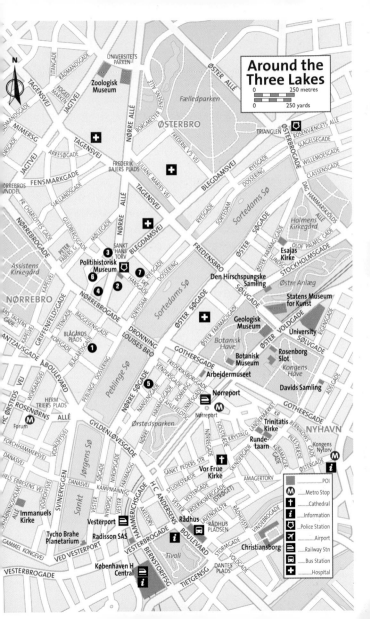

W www.botanik.snm.ku.dk **L** Gardens 08.30–18.00 Mon–Sun,
May–Sept; 08.30–16.00 Tues–Sun, Oct–Apr, Museum 12.00–16.00
Mon–Sun, June–Aug **N** Bus 5A, 6A, 14, 350S; metro/S-train: Nørreport

Fælledparken

To the northeast of trendy Nørrebro is this expansive green area. It
has a classy skateboarding park, an open-air pool, children's play areas,
imaginative planting and a good café. It is also home to the huge
National Stadium **a** Parken, Øster Allé 50 **t** 35437400 **W** www.fck.dk.
There are often free concerts here and many impromptu football games.
A good place for a break from the city centre, where you can join ordinary
Danes in enjoying some leisure time. **N** Bus: 1A, 3A, 42, 184, 185, 150S

Kongens Have (Royal Gardens)

Copenhagen's oldest park, created as the private gardens of
Christian IV when he built Rosenborg Slot and laid out in a series
of grids that can still be observed today. It's full of huge old trees,
with a pretty hedged garden and a pond full of very self-satisfied
ducks. A popular spot for sunbathing and picnicking, and a good
café. Kids will love the playground and puppet theatre in summer.
a Gothersgade **W** www.ses.dk **L** 07.00–17.00 Dec & Jan;
07.00–18.00 Feb & Nov; 07.00–19.00 Mar & Oct; 07.00–21.00 Apr;
07.00–22.00 May–Sept **N** Bus: 350S; metro/S-train: Nørreport

Nansensgade

This is one of Copenhagen's delightful quarters that often goes
undiscovered by tourists. The village-like atmosphere on this street
is not to be missed – you can easily spend a few hours here wandering
around the small clothes shops and home-furnishing boutiques.
There are plenty of bars – check out the freaky and popular Bankerot,

🔺 *Fountain in Kongens Have, with Cupid on a swan*

meaning 'bankrupt'. Some of the city's best pizzerias and ice cream parlours are here. Ⓝ Bus: 2A, 5A; metro/S-train: Nørreport

Rosenborg Slot (Rosenborg Castle)

Lovely, popular little castle built by Christian IV , telling the history of the Danish kings from the 16th to the 19th century. The place was built in the 17th century by Christian IV as a summer palace and from the 18th century, when one of the King Frederiks built a bigger home at Frederiksborg, it was used to store the royal heirlooms. You can see the royal tableware, including glass knives and forks, a solid silver table, huge silver lions and heaps of portraits, all chronologically arranged as you walk around the palace. The dazzling crown jewels are in the basement. Busy at peak times. Ⓐ Øster Voldgade 4a Ⓣ 33153286 Ⓛ 11.00–18.00 Tues–Sun, Jan–Apr; 11.00–16.00 Mon–Sun, May; 10.00–17.00 Mon–Sun, June–Aug; 10.00–16.00 Mon–Sun, Sept & Oct; 11.00–16.00 Tues–Sun, Nov & Dec Ⓝ Bus: 5A, 6A, 350S; metro/S-train: Nørreport

Rundetaarn

Another of Christian IV's creations, Rundetaarn was completed in 1642. The tower is part of the 'Trinitatis complex' and linked to an observatory, a student church and a university library. It has a unique 209 m (686 ft) spiral ramp and a short narrow stairwell to the very top. As well as being the oldest functioning observatory in Europe, the tower often holds interesting art and photo exhibitions, seminars and conferences, and classical music concerts. Fantastic views over the rooftops of the Copenhagen. Ⓐ Købmagergade 52a Ⓣ 33730373 Ⓦ www.rundetaarn.dk Ⓔ post@rundetaarn.dk Ⓛ 10.00–20.00 Mon–Sat, 12.00–20.00 Sun, June–Sept; 10.00–17.00 Mon–Sat, 12.00–17.00 Sun, Oct–May Ⓝ Bus: 6A, 5A; metro/S-train: Nørreport

⬥ *Architecture straight out of Hans Christian Andersen – Rosenborg Slot*

Sankt Hans Torv

The centre of cool Nørrebro, Sankt Hans Torv is a small square
which forms the junction of several intersecting streets. Fælledvej,
Elmegade and Guldbergsgade are home to some of the city's best
eateries, bars and night haunts and quirky, local fashion boutiques.
This area is where all the really tuned-in Copenhageners hang
out, including assorted younger royals. In summer afternoons the
pavement tables fill with the chattering classes and the evenings
are enlivened with clubbers. Ⓝ Bus: 3A, 5A, 350S

CULTURE

Arbejdermuseet (Workers Museum)

No Danish design items in this engaging little museum dedicated
to the working lives of Copenhagen's citizens. Progressing through
the various incarnations of Danish home life, this encapsulates
the hardship of many of the city's working people in a series of
recreated rooms. Text is only in Danish but the images are graphic
enough to tell the story well. Overcrowding and poverty give way
gradually to comfort with the few essential items of the 19th century
(an overturned table for a bed, primitive contraceptives, cheap,
ineffective medicines) replaced by gramophones, washing machines,
table lamps and three-piece suites. Recreated in its entirety is the
apartment of the Sørenson family, unaltered from 1915 to 1990,
when the daughter finally gave everything to the museum. The café
is another traditional Copenhagen construct, selling traditional food
and drinks. ⓐ Rømersgade 22 ⓘ 33932575 Ⓦ www.arbejdermuseet.dk
🕐 10.00–16.00 Ⓝ Bus: 5A, 14, 1 40, 42, 150S, 350S; metro/S-train:
Nørreport. Admission charge

● *The Hirschsprung Collection has an intimate, domestic setting*

Den Hirschsprungske Samling (Hirschsprung Collection)

Denmark's finest collection of 19th- and early 20th-century Danish art was tobacco manufacturer Heinrich Hirschsprung's gift to the Danish State, with the pre-condition that it be housed in an intimate setting. The neo-classical building contains a series of small rooms where exhibits are displayed, designed to reproduce their original setting in the German–Jewish immigrant's own home. The collection includes works by Danish artist C W Eckberg and his students Christian Købke and William Bende. The gallery is often forgotten by visitors in the art overload of its neighbour, the Statens Museum for Kunst. Check out the tobacco theme in the lobby with the mosaic floor and the portrait of the city's benefactor. ⓐ Stockholmsgade 20 ⓣ 35420336 ⓦ www.hirschsprung.dk ⓛ 11.00–16.00 Wed–Mon, closed Tues ⓝ Bus: 6A, 150S, 14, 40, 184, 185 to Sølvtorvet; S-train: Nørreport Station

STATENS MUSEUM FOR KUNST (NATIONAL GALLERY)
This was originally the private art collection of the Danish royals, who decided to let the nation share their treasures. The permanent collection covers seven centuries of painting. A stunning modern extension at the back, designed by Danish architect Anna Maria Indrio, now houses temporary exhibitions of statuary. The huge glass north wall of the museum forms a panoramic rural scene in summer. There is a children's section, regular concerts and performances in the new foyer, changing exhibitions and a good café and bookshop. ⓐ Sølvgade 48 ⓣ 33748494 ⓦ www.smk.dk ⓛ 10.00–17.00 Tues & Thur–Sun, 10.00–20.00 Wed ⓝ Bus: 14, 40

Zoologisk Museum (Zoological Museum)

Not to be confused with the actual zoo beside Frederiksberg Slot (see page 83), this museum is for stuffed creatures only. One section is dedicated to animals that have adapted to urban living, while others contain massive walruses, a 14 m (46 ft) long skeleton of a bowhead whale, polar bears and lots of insects. There is also a children's section. ⓐ Universitetsparken 15 ⓣ 35321001 ⓦ www.zoologi.snm.ku.dk ⓔ zm@snm.ku.dk ⓛ 11.00–17.00 Tues–Sun ⓝ Bus: 18, 150S. Admission charge

RETAIL THERAPY

There is much to see and buy in the area around the Three Lakes, chiefly to the north in hip Nørrebro. Blågårdsgade and Elmegade have a bohemian atmosphere and are full of alternative shops.

There is a Saturday flea market along the yellow wall of the Assistens Kirkegård and another at Israel Plads close to Nørreport station. Frederiksborggade has designer clothes and home accessory shops. Ravensborggade is literally lined with antique shops – **Montan Antik Design** at no. 17 and **Veirhanen** at no. 12 are worth searching out.

TAKING A BREAK

Café Flora £ ❶ Popular spot to brunch or lunch. Order anything on the menu to take away. ➋ Blågårdsgade 27 ❶ 35390018 Ⓦ www.floraskaffebar.dk ❶ 10.00–24.00 Mon–Wed, 10.00–01.00 Thur–Sat, 10.00–23.00 Sun ❷ Bus: 5A

Picnic £ ❷ Organic *meze*-style lunch. Eat in or take away. ➋ Fælledvej 22b ❶ 35390953 ❶ 11.00–23.00 Mon–Fri, 10.30–23.00 Sat & Sun ❷ Bus: 5A, 350S

Café Sebastopol £–££ ❸ Trendy French-style café, excellent breakfasts and lunches. Order at the bar. ➋ Sankt Hans Torv 2 ❶ 35363002 Ⓦ www.sebastopol.dk ❶ 08.00–01.00 Mon–Wed, 08.00–02.00 Thur & Fri, 09.00–02.00 Sat, 09.00–01.00 Sun ❷ Bus: 5A, 350S

Gefährlich ££ ❹ This two-storey cultural melting pot houses a hairdresser, restaurant, art gallery, coffee shop, record store and bar and nightclub. Serving good coffee, exciting cocktails, breakfast, lunch and dinner, visit this place at any time of the day and enjoy the creative artistic extras. ➋ Fælledvej 7 ❶ 35241324 ❷ Bus: 5A, 350S

AFTER DARK

RESTAURANTS

Bibendum ££ ❺ Serving only tapas, cheese and charcuterie, Bibendum is famed for its fantastic wine collection with over 50 varieties served by the glass. Reservation recommended in evening. ⓐ Nansensgade 45 ❶ 33330774 Ⓦ www.vincafe.dk ⓔ info@vincafe.dk Ⓛ 16.00–24.00 Mon–Sat Ⓝ Bus: 5A, 6A, 14, 350S; S-train: Nørreport

The Laundromat Café ££ ❻ Trendy retro café, and yes, it really is a laundry. Loungy music. ⓐ Elmegade 15 ❶ 35352672 Ⓛ 08.00–24.00 Mon–Thur, 10.00–02.00 Fri & Sat Ⓝ Bus: 5A, 350S

Nørrebro Bryghus ££ ❼ Restaurant and microbrewery with excellent modern European cuisine and 12 different beers, all brewed on site. Waiters will offer their recommendations or you can try the sampler. ⓐ Ryesgade 3 ❶ 35300530 Ⓦ www.norrebrobryghus.dk Ⓛ 11.00–24.00 Mon–Wed, 11.00–02.00 Thur–Sat, 10.00–22.00 Sun Ⓝ Bus: 5A, 350S

CLUBS

Rust One of the liveliest clubs and live music venues in town, with two floors and three small bars. Over 21s only. ⓐ Guldbergsgade 8 ❶ 35245200 Ⓦ www.rust.dk Ⓛ 21.00–05.00 Wed–Sat. Admission charge for nightclub and some concerts Ⓝ Bus: 5A, 350S

Stengade 30 Alternative music. Tuesday is open mike night. Check the website for what's on. ⓐ Stengade 18 ❶ 35360938 Ⓦ www.stengade30.dk ⓔ stengade30@stengade30.dk Ⓝ Bus: 5A, 350S

---

❿ *Zealand's beaches are only a short trip from the capital*

The Øresund Coast

Copenhagen lies on the eastern side of the island of Zealand, or 'Sjælland'. Along its northeastern shore, served by an efficient *Kystbanen* rail service, lies the Danish Riviera which faces out onto Øresund. To take in all of the sights you need a few days, but you can mix and match if time is short.

Elsinor, or 'Helsingør' is the furthest point on this trip at 47 km (29 miles) from Copenhagen, about 1 hour 15 minutes by train. Before that, you'll find the Louisiana Museum of Modern Art in Humlebæk (45 minutes by train), Bakken Amusement Park (20 minutes) and Charlottenlund (15 minutes) with its beaches and the Akvarium. The Experimentarium is just outside Copenhagen in Hellerup. The open-air Frilandsmuseet (Frilands Museum) is great for children.

SIGHTS & ATTRACTIONS

Charlottenlund Beach & Danmarks Akvarium

The Danish Riviera begins at Charlottenlund Beach, a popular, scenic green area with a tiny strip of sand and nice views over Copenhagen harbour. To one side is a private bathing area with its own café, toilets and showers and separate nude bathing places for men and women. There is also a picnic area. Close by are the remains of Charlottenlund Fort, now a campsite.

Most visitors come for the Akvarium, with over 300 species of fish and water creatures, including piranhas, crocodiles, sharks and a coelacanth preserved in alcohol. You can watch the feeding times and at weekends and public holidays there are touch pools.

ⓐ Kavalergården 1 ❶ 39623283 ⓦ www.akvarium.dk ❶ 10.00–18.00

BAKKEN AMUSEMENT PARK & BELLEVUE BEACH

Founded in 1583, Bakken Amusement Park lays claim to being the oldest in the world. Popular with Copenhagen families since the 35 rides are bigger and cheaper than Tivoli and admission to the park itself is free. There are beer halls, gaming arcades, a shooting gallery, and at night a popular revue show, together with lots of cafés and restaurants.

Next door is Jægersborg Dyrehaven, a vast expanse of parkland with free roaming deer. Close by is Bellevue beach, a popular sunbathing spot with open green spaces, good eating and clear water. Look out for the Arne Jacobsen influence in the area, particularly the petrol station ⓐ Dyrehavsbakken, Dyrehavej 62, Klampenborg ⓣ 39962096 ⓦ www.bakken.dk ⓛ Mar–Aug, times vary so check website ⓝ S train or Kystbanen to Klampenborg. Admission charge for rides

May–Aug; 10.00–17.00 Feb–Apr, Sept & Oct; 10.00–16.00 Nov–Jan ⓝ S-train: Charlottenlund. Admission charge

Experimentarium

Northeast of Østerbro in Hellerup lies the Experimentarium. This is a hands-on science centre housed in the former Tuborg bottling factory, and it is great for kids. The centre offers piloted tours explaining the various aspects of science which affect our lives. All the exhibits are designed to get people involved, from gyroscopes to making cheese to wandering through a hall of mirrors. The exhibits change regularly but there are constant troops of children storming around. The afternoon is generally quieter. ⓐ Tuborg Havnevej 7 ⓣ 39273333

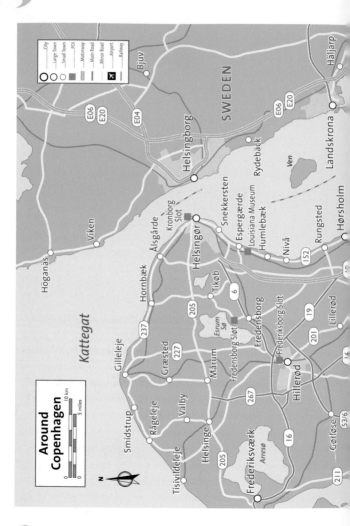

Around
Copenhagen

City
Large Town
Small Town
PCH
Motorway
Main Road
Minor Road
Airport
Railway

SWEDEN

Kattegat

Häljarp
Bjuv
Helsingborg
Landskrona
Rydebäck
Ven
Viken
Höganäs
Snekkersten
Espergærde
Louisiana Museum
Humlebæk
Nivå
Rungsted
Hørsholm
Kronborg Slot
Helsingør
Ålsgårde
Hornbæk
Tikøb
Esrum Sø
Fredensborg
Fredensborg Slot
Frederiksborg Slot
Lillerød
Gilleleje
Græsted
Mårum
Hillerød
Rågeleje
Valby
Helsinge
Frederiksværk
Arresø
Gørløse
Smidstrup
Tisvildeleje

E06 E20
E04
E06 E20
152
6
205
237
227
267
205
16
201
19
53/6
211

N

0 10 km
0 5 miles

118

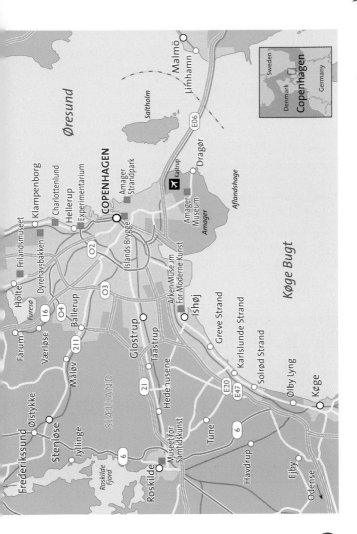

Ⓦ www.experimentarium.dk Ⓔ info@experimentarium.dk
Ⓛ 09.30–17.00 Mon & Wed–Fri, 09.30–21.00 Tues, 11.00–17.00
Sat & Sun Ⓝ Bus: 1A; S-train: Hellerup. Admission charge

Helsingør & Kronborg Slot (Kronborg Castle)

Kronborg Castle, Shakespeare's setting for *Hamlet*, was originally
a large toll collection point for ships entering the narrow Øresund.
It became a castle in 1574, when Frederick II took a liking to the spot.
Burned down by accident in 1629, rebuilt and then ravaged by the
Swedes in 1658, it was again restored in 1922. You can now visit the
Danish Maritime Museum, the king's chambers, the chapel and
the dungeons. The chief draw is the king's quarters, a complete
fabrication but with genuine artefacts brought in from other
sites. The ship museum is interesting, as is the pretty, completely
reconstructed, chapel, but the dungeon is a real horror – don't go
there if you are at all claustrophobic. The real highlight is the

🔺 *Kronborg Castle – Elsinore without Hamlet*

building itself, set on a promontory of land and looking very much as though Hamlet could pop up on the battlements at any moment.

The rest of Helsingør contains, as well as lots of Swedes who flock here for the (relatively) cheaper alcohol, antique shops and an excellent town museum. Just northwest of town is Marienlyst Slot, an 18th-century manor house with exhibits of local paintings and silverware.

Helsingør Bymuseum ⓐ Sankt Anna Gade 36 ⓣ 49281800
Ⓦ www.visithelsingor.dk Ⓛ 12.00–16.00. Admission charge
Kronborg Slot ⓐ Kronborg 2 ⓣ 49213078 Ⓦ www.kronborgslot.dk
Ⓛ 10.30–17.00 May–Sept; 11.00–16.00 Tues–Sun, Apr & Oct;
11.00–15.00 Tues–Sun, Nov–Mar. Admission charge
Marienlyst Slot ⓐ Marienlyst Allé 32 ⓣ 49281830 Ⓦ www.helsingor.dk
Ⓛ 12.00–16.00. Admission charge

CULTURE

Louisiana Museum of Modern Art

Don't miss a visit to this superb modern art museum, founded in 1954 by a private collector, Knud Jensen, in a 19th-century villa on the Øresund. Helped by funding from the Carlsberg Foundation, it is now a circular series of single-storey galleries around a garden of amazing statues. The huge glass walls of many of the galleries give the impression that galleries, garden and sea are all part of one strangely lit, complex whole. The weather and the sea play an enormous part in how you experience the exhibits.

The collection includes works by Lichtenstein, Warhol and Oldenburg, and also Picasso, Francis Bacon, Giacometti and Rothko. There is also art by a group of left-wing abstract artists formed in 1948 known as the CoBrA movement after the first letters of the

names of their home cities (Copenhagen, Brussels and Amsterdam). In the garden, Henry Moore's *Bronze Woman* and statues by Max Ernst, Alexander Calder, Joan Miró and Giacometti sit in their own corners. There is an indoor children's area where kids can take part in art workshops and a clever playground in the garden. You will also find an excellent café and shop. ❷ Gammel Strandvej 1, Humlebæk ❶ 49 19 07 19 ❿ www.louisiana.dk ❶ 10.00–17.00 Mon, Tues & Thurs–Sun, 10.00–22.00 Wed ❷ Kystbanen to Humlebæk. Admission charge, free for under 18s

RETAIL THERAPY

The museum shop at Louisiana, aside from the usual postcards, books and ornaments, has great soft furnishings and clothes. Kronborg Castle has good souvenirs and Christmas decorations, glassware and hand-woven garments.

The three main pedestrianised shopping streets in Helsingør are Stengade, Stjernegade and Bjergegade. Along Bjergegade check

⬇ *Pop-art heaven at the Louisiana*

out **Baagø**, an enormous butcher and delicatessen. **Lynhjems Eftf Ole Jensen** in Stengade sells more cheeses than you thought existed. **Crepandia** is an interesting toy store in the same street and **Vin Og Stoger** at no. 17 is an antique shop full of curiosities.

TAKING A BREAK

Axeltorv square in Helsingør is a scruffy square filled with shoppers, cheap cafés and bars and some budget restaurants. For a nicer meal you might try:

Solarium Café £–££ in the Louisiana museum. Overlooks the sea, with outside tables surrounded by garden statuary. ⓐ Louisiana Museum, Gammel Strandvej 1, Humlebæk ☉ 49190719 ☉ 10.00–16.30 Mon, Tues & Thur–Sun, 10.00–21.30 Wed

Madam Sprunck ££–£££ An old-fashioned French-style café, bar and restaurant set in a pretty courtyard. Voted Helsingør's best spot in 2006. A 'tasting' menu allows you to sample five dishes. ⓐ Stengade 48, Helsingør ☉ 49264849 ☉ 11.30–24.00 Mon–Thur, 11.30–02.00 Fri, 10.30–02.00 Sat, 10.30–24.00 Sun

If you are out for the day at Bakken there are over 35 cafés and restaurants to choose from and plenty of places for a picnic lunch. In Klampenborg, the town where you alight for Bakken, try:

Peter Liep Hus £–££ Beautiful thatched roofed house with an interesting history. Outdoor tables for sunny days and good children's menu. ⓐ Dyrehaven 8, Klampenborg ☉ 39640786 ⓦ www.peterliep.dk ☉ 11.00–21.00 Tues–Sun

Restaurant Jacobsen £££ Designed by Arne Jacobsen as part of the Bellavista theatre and housing complex. One for a special occasion. ❸ Strandvejen 449, Klampenborg ❶ 39634322 ❼ www.restaurantjacobsen.dk ❻ 12.00–24.00 Mon–Fri, 11.00–22.00 Sat, 11.00–21.00 Sun; closed Sun, Oct–Apr

ACCOMMODATION

Danhostel Helsingor ££ Hostel set in an old manor house 2 km (1.5 miles) northwest of Helsingør. En suite double rooms and dorms Pleasant nearby beach. ❸ Ndr Strandvej 24, Helsingør ❶ 49211640 ❼ www.helsingorhostel.dk ❷ Bus: 340 or local train to Højstrup Trinbræt

Hotel Hamlet £££ Good restaurant, nice rooms and some old-world charm. ❸ Bramstræde 5, Helsingør ❶ 49210591 ❼ www.hotelhamlet.dk

Hotel Marienlyst £££+ Hotel, casino and spa with views across to Sweden or Kronborg and two top restaurants and bars. ❸ Ndr Strandvej 2, Helsingør ❶ 49214000 ❼ www.marienlyst.dk

Roskilde & Hillerød

Roskilde, 30 minutes from the city by train, was once the capital of
Denmark and has a deal more bustle about it. Its biggest attractions
are the Viking Ship Museum and the cathedral, where generations
of Danish kings and queens are at rest. Hillerød is a pretty little
inland town about 40 minutes from Copenhagen by train,
dominated by the fairytale lakeside castle of Frederiksborg.
Trains to both towns run at frequent intervals from Copenhagen
Central Station. See map on page 118.

ROSKILDE

SIGHTS & ATTRACTIONS
Museet for Samtidskunst (Museum of Contemporary Art)
Located in the town square of Roskilde and housed in the
Palæsamlingerne, a former 18th-century palace, the art here
is seriously contemporary. The museum was nominated
Museum of the Year in 2003. ❸ Stændertorvet 3d ❶ 46316570
Ⓦ www.samtidskunst.dk ❶ 11.00–17.00 Tues–Fri, 12.00–16.00
Sat & Sun. Admission charge

Roskilde Domkirke (Cathedral)
A wooden church was first built on this site during the 11th century
by a man with the curious, yet oddly modern, name of Harold
Bluetooth (Harald Blaatand). In 1170 Bishop Absalon ordered
a cathedral to be built, and the east section of the church was
completed by the mid-13th century. The rest is an amalgam of

● *Roskilde is dominated by its sober and impressive Cathedral*

VIKING SHIP MUSEUM

See the workshops, where full-size working versions of
Viking ships are made, the museum island, where hardy
young men and women hack out longboats made from
planks or hollowed out trunks by hand, using original tools,
and the finished boats themselves, fitted out for sea. Around
the workshops are young trees of the species used in the
longboats, and a few stalls have activities for children. There
are sometimes demonstrations of the boats themselves,

● *Nothing matches the thrill of seeing a real Viking ship*

which handle a little as if Laurel and Hardy were sailing them but get under way eventually.

The museum displays five Viking ships found in Roskilde harbour, lovingly reconstructed against a huge glass wall looking out over the harbour. If you or your children fancy it, you can put on Viking clothes and stand inside a mocked-up trading ship or play Viking board games. Good shop.

ⓐ Vindeboder 12 ① 46300300 Ⓦ www.vikingeskibsmuseet.dk
① 10.00–17.00. Admission charge

later additions made over the following 800 years, and you can clearly see the different parts.

The cathedral is a world heritage site and its particular interest, other than its architecture, lies in the side chapels built by various monarchs to hold their mortal remains. On entering the cathedral pick up one of the handouts that list the various side chapels and their occupants. Some of the sarcophagi are plain, austere boxes while others wouldn't be out of place in Tivoli Gardens.

There is also an amusing clock that depicts St George slaying the dragon on the hour, and a 1554 working organ. Upstairs is a museum charting the history of the cathedral, its centrepiece being a replica of a dress worn by Margarethe I (1375–1412). ⓐ Domkirke Pladsen ⓣ 46355814 ⓦ www.roskildedomkirke.dk ⓛ 09.00–17.00 Mon–Sat, 12.30–17.00 Sun, Apr–Sept; 10.00–16.00 Tues–Sat, 12.30–16.00 Sun, Oct–Mar. Admission charge, under sevens free

Roskilde Museum

Near to the Palæsamlingerne and accessible using the same entrance ticket is the main branch of the museum. It charts the history of Roskilde from prehistoric times right up to the Roskilde music festival. ⓐ Sankt Olsgade 15 & 18 ⓣ 46316500 ⓦ www.roskildemuseum.dk ⓛ 11.00–16.00. Admission charge

RETAIL THERAPY

Shopping in Roskilde, mostly on pedestrianised streets, has a quietly suburban feel to it. The shopping streets are largely for pedestrians only, and there are tables out on the pavements with busy shoppers taking a break. At Rosenhavestrædet 2, **Strædet 2** sells some pretty clothes and soft furnishings. Algade has several interesting shops. At no. 37 you'll find **Butik Jane Onø**, selling all sorts of coffee beans, crockery, candles, cushions, light fittings, perfume, marmalade, chocolates. Check out **Tiger**, a chain store where everything costs 10kr or 20kr.

The Viking Ship Museum sells Viking-related souvenirs. In an old gasworks building beside it are two great shops: **Glassgalleriet** (🅰 Sankt Ibsvej 12 🆆 www.glasgalleriet.dk), a craft shop where the pieces, all glass, are hand-made on the premises, and **Roskildegalleriet** (🅰 Hedegade 1 🆆 www.roskildegalleriet.dk), a warren of galleries selling the work of local artists.

TAKING A BREAK

Next door to Strædet 2 on Rosenhavestrædet is the pleasant **Café Satchmo**, good for a cup of coffee and Danish before setting off for the cathedral. In Skomagergade, the pedestrianised street south of the cathedral, you'll find any number of pleasant places to stop for a break.

Restaurant Raadhuskælderen £–££ In a cellar by the old town hall, the interior combines the antique feel, with arched windows and brick walls, with modern seating and good lighting. Seating outside in summer. 🅰 Fondens Bro 1 ☎ 46360100 🆆 www.raadhuskaelderen.dk 🕐 11.00–23.00, Kitchen open 11.30–16.00 and 17.00–21.30

AFTER DARK

For a lively weekend, come the last weekend in June for the four-day Roskilde Music Festival.

Snekken £–££ Close to the Viking Ship Museum and overlooking Roskilde harbour, with outdoor tables in summer and Danish-Mediterranean-style food. 🅰 Vindeboder 16 ☎ 46359816

ⓦ www.snekken.dk **🕐** 11.00–23.00, Kitchen open 11.30–16.30
and 18.30–21.30

Gourmethuset Store Børs £££–£££ A fantastic kitchen and homebrewed
beer. Choose à la carte or a set menu of anything from two to seven
courses. **ⓐ** Havnevej 43 **☏** 46325045 **ⓦ** www.store-bors.dk
🕐 12.00–23.00, Kitchen open 17.00–21.30

ACCOMMODATION

Roskilde Vandrerhjem £ Ultra-modern hostel with en suite double
rooms, family rooms, and views of the harbour. Cooking facilities.
ⓐ Vindeboder 7, Roskilde **☏** 46352184 **ⓦ** www.danhostel.dk

Hotel Prindsen £££ Supposedly Denmark's oldest hotel. Lots of charm.
ⓐ Algade 13, Roskilde **☏** 46309100 **ⓦ** www.hotelprindsen.dk

HILLERØD

SIGHTS & ATTRACTIONS
Frederiksborg Slot

Dramatic building set on a series of islands in a man-made lake and
surrounded by gardens. Like Rosenborg (see page 108), the site was
a summer palace, built in 1560 by Frederik II. Christian IV later added
a bigger structure in the Dutch Renaissance style from a design by
Hans van Steenwinckel.

In the open courtyard, don't miss the Neptune Fountain,
a 19th-century replica of the original that was destroyed during the
Swedish occupation. The main body of the castle, destroyed first by
the Swedes and then by fire in 1859, is now a museum funded by
the Carlsberg Foundation. It charts the history of the Danish royal

family, with a series of paintings of moments from Denmark's history and portraits of the kings and queens. The chapel, where Danish kings were crowned for nearly two centuries, survived the fire and the Swedes intact and is stunningly ornate, especially when the sun bursts through the stained glass. In the reconstructed Great Hall, look up at the artwork on the ceiling.

The third floor is a national portrait gallery, including a portrait of the present queen by Andy Warhol. Take a look out of the windows along the northeast wall of the house for beautiful views over the baroque garden. ☎ 48260439 ⓦ www.frederiksborgmuseet.dk ⏰ 10.00–17.00 Apr–Oct; 11.00–15.00 Nov–Mar. Admission charge

RETAIL THERAPY

In Hillerød, close by the castle is a craft shop selling patterned jumpers, pottery and the like. The castle shop is well worth a browse too. Slotsgade is a pedestrianised shopping area and the parallel street Herredsvejen contains the shopping centre Slotsarkaderne.

TAKING A BREAK

Spisestedet Leonora £–££ Located in the castle grounds, this is a convenient stop for lunch à la carte. Danish menu. ☎ 48267516 ⓦ www.leonora.dk ⏰ 10.00–17.00, Kitchen open 11.00–16.00

Slotskroen ££ Traditional Danish buffet lunch. ⓐ Slotsgade 67 ☎ 48201800 ⓦ www.slotskroen.dk ⏰ Sat & Sun only

AFTER DARK

Den Gale Coq £ This is a good option for an evening meal. ⓐ Helsingørsgade 16 ☎ 48267545

Amager

The route from the airport into town by train seems to be a series of building sites as the countryside to the south and east of Copenhagen is developed. The places of interest to tourists in this area are on the flat, culturally distinct island of Amager. This island is linked to Copenhagen by a series of bridges, and now to Malmö in Sweden by Øresundsbroen (Øresund Bridge).

Aside from the airport, Amager is home to Denmark's largest shopping centre, Fields, and the national radio and TV station Danmarks Radio (DR). As yet it's still a nice quiet area, with good beaches along the eastern coastline, a big nature reserve on the western side and some pretty villages, in particular Dragør.

On the western side on reclaimed land is **Kalvebod Faelled** (or Western Amager), a huge nature reserve created during World War II to provide work for Danish men who might otherwise have been transported to Germany to work in the munitions factories. It was used for many years as a firing range before the wildlife park was created. An interpretive centre for the nature reserve offers bikes for hire and use of a campsite in the reserve.

Closer to town is Islands Brygge, a suburb of Copenhagen with an outdoor swimming pool and some nice walks along the waterfront.

SIGHTS & ATTRACTIONS

Amager Museum
Folk museum showing the life and history of Dutch settlers in the 16th century. Set in two old Dutch farms, the museum grows vegetables in the old style, while its curators, dressed in traditional clothes, show you farm processes from cheese and butter making to looking after the

animals. The museum is en route to Dragør by road. ❷ Hovedgade 4 & 12, Store Magleby ❶ 32530250 ❷ 12.00–16.00 Tues–Sun, May–Sept; 12.00–16.00 Wed & Sun, Oct–Apr ❷ Bus: 30, 73. Admission charge

Amager Strandpark

There has been a beach on Amager's east coast since the 1930s and recreational activities have been going on there for even longer. In the mid-1990s, plans were made to develop the area into a new *Strandpark* (beach park).

Opened officially in August 2005, this 4.6 km (2.9 miles) futuristic beach boasts an impressive island and lagoon where you will often see kayakers warming up before heading out to sea. In the middle of the island are five 'stations', small innovative designer concrete buildings equipped with spacious and clean toilet and shower facilities, including facilities for the disabled. From the roof there is a fantastic view over the Øresund region.

The northern side of the lagoon is made up of artificial sand dunes while the southern side has a large park for picnics and barbeques. The entire area is protected for recreation purposes only and in summer the place is filled with beach volleyball, kayakers, joggers, basketball matches, puppet shows and more. ❶ 33663336 ❷ www.amager-strand.dk ❷ mail@amager-strand.dk ❷ Facilities 08.00–20.00 Apr–May; 08.00–22.00 June–Aug ❷ Metro: Lergravsparken, Øresund & Amager Strand

Dragør

If you want to experience at first hand a complete Danish community in all its *hygge* (cosiness) a good place to visit is the tiny cobbled village of Dragør on the east coast of Amager. Picture-postcard perfect, the village seems fixed in a little time capsule where

◆ The startling Ark Museum of Modern Art

ARKEN MUSEUM

The Arken Museum for Moderne Kunst (The Ark Museum of Modern Art) is 17 km (11 miles) west of Amager in the working-class suburb of Ishøj, and is a highlight of the area.

Standing on an inaccessible windswept beach reclaimed from Køge Bay, this disorientating museum opened to much acclaim and controversy during Copenhagen's year as European City of Culture in 1996. Designed by architect Søren Robert Lund to look like a giant beached concrete and steel ship, it has a startling effect when viewed from a distance.

The museum has a permanent collection but its chief exhibits are temporary displays, often of very contemporary works, including cinema. Check the website for what's currently on.

The restaurant on the first floor has great views over the bay. The gallery stands on a long reclaimed beach between the towns of Brøndby and Hundige, and is an excellent place for a quiet afternoon.

The museum is easily accessible by public transport. See the map on page 118. 🚇 Skovvej 100, Ishøj 🕿 43540222 🌐 www.arken.dk 📧 reception@arken.dk 🕒 10.00–17.00 Tues & Thur–Sun, 10.00–21.00 Wed 🚆 S-train: A or E to Ishøj, then bus: 128. Admission charge

hollyhocks and tiny pruned bay trees are tended in the cracks between houses and cobbles and the heat of the sun glows off the orange tiled roofs. The village prospered in the 14th century as a fishing port. When steam and diesel powered ships made the sea

trade uneconomical for small fishermen, the village emptied and remained untouched for a century or so until improved transport links brought it back into use. The village square is fronted with houses dating back to the late 18th century, while the obelisk at its centre marks the distance from Copenhagen as one and a half Danish miles. There is a tiny museum close to the harbour containing seafaring memorabilia and a history of the village. The best time to visit Dragør is the last weekend in July or beginning of August for the annual music festival (🌐 www.dragoermusikfest.dk). Museum ⓐ Havnepladsen Strandlinien 2 ☎ 32534106 🕐 12.00–16.00 Tues–Sun, May–Sept 🚍 Bus: 30, 32, 73, 350S. Admission charge

Islands Brygge

Walking distance from Rådhuspladsen and Christianshavn, this suburb of the city is rapidly taking on a bohemian atmosphere with lots of art galleries opening up. Along Sturlasgade, look up **Galleri Christina Wilson** (no. 12h), **GIMM E15** (no. 14d), **I-N-K** (no. 21h), **Nils Stæk** (no. 19c) and **Galleri Nicolai Wallner** (no. 21). This area also holds one of Copenhagen's harbour pools, and has its own cultural centre along the waterside. 🌐 www.islands-brygge.com 🚍 Bus: 33, 40; metro to Islands Brygge

RETAIL THERAPY

Det Blå Pakhus Copenhagen's largest indoor flea market. Hundreds of stalls of second-hand goods, bric-a-brac and antiques. ⓐ Holmbladsgade 113, Amager ☎ 32951707 🌐 www.blaapakhus.dk 🕐 10.00–17.00 Sat & Sun 🚍 Bus: 2A, 5A, 350S; Metro: Amagerbro

Retrograd Retro items for the home, used and new. Fun to browse.
⊙ Gunløgsgade 7, Islands Brygge ❶ 22414657 ◷ 12.00–17.00 Mon,
12.00–19.00 Tues–Fri

TAKING A BREAK & AFTER DARK

There's not much to keep you after dark in Amager. Instead, a short
metro ride from the beach and Islands Brygge into the city will take
you to the bars and restaurants around Kongen's Nytorv. At Amager
beach a few multicoloured beach bars offer drinks and snacks, as do
the five concrete stations.

Café Alma £ Good coffee and light meals, including a good vegetarian
option and home-made cakes. ⊙ Isafjordsgade 5–7, Islands Brygge
❶ 32543204 ◷ 11.00–24.00 Mon–Thur, 11.00–01.30 Fri, 10.00–01.30
Sat, 10.00–24.00 Sun ⊗ Bus: 5A; Metro: Islands Brygge

⬤ Islands Brygge is laid-back, even by Copenhagen standards

Café Saga £ Recently voted best new café of 2005, this place in the bohemian quarter of Islands Brygge has sunny outdoor seating and reasonable prices. ❸ Egilsgade 20, Islands Brygge ❶ 32571724 ● 11.00–24.00 Mon–Fri, 10.00–24.00 Sat, 10.00–22.00 Sun ❷ Bus: 5A; Metro: Islands Brygge

Beghuset ££ Reputedly the best that Dragør has to offer. Comfortable Danish–French cooking and lots of locals. ❸ Standgade 14, Dragør ❶ 32530136 ● 11.30–late, Kitchen open 12.00–15.00 & 18.00–21.30 Tues–Sat, 12.00–15.00 Sun ❷ Bus 350S

Krunch Restauraunt Kastrup Fortet ££ Organic restaurant with views over Amager beach and the Øresund. ❸ Amager Strandvej 246 ❶ 32845050 ❿ www.krunch.dk ❸ mail@krunch.dk ● 12.00–16.00 & 17.00–22.00 ❷ Bus: 2A; Metro: Lergravsparken

ACCOMMODATION

Many of the interesting sights on Amager are a short metro or bus ride from the city, so it is advisable to stay in the centre to make the most of your trip. If you fancy a night or two out of town, the best option is the 100-year-old **Dragør Badehotel ££** ❸ Drogdensvej 43, Dragør ❶ 32530500 ❿ www.badehotellet.dk ❷ Bus: 350S

● *Not all the police carry light sabres!*

Directory

GETTING THERE

By air

Ticketless budget airlines are often the cheapest way to travel, especially if you fly off peak. You will find prices are lower the earlier you book; a ticket booked the day before you leave will cost much more than one on the same flight booked weeks in advance. Prices go up during holidays, at weekends and when there is an event on in Copenhagen.

British airports, including London, Birmingham, Manchester, Aberdeen, Glasgow and Edinburgh, have direct flights to Copenhagen, as does Dublin. Flying time from London airports is around 1 hour 45 minutes.

There is a direct link by metro (15 mins), bus (30 mins) or train (15 mins) to the city centre.

Ryanair flies from London Stansted and Luton to Malmö in Sweden, which is only a 30-minute road or rail journey from Copenhagen. Airlines offering flights to Copenhagen include:

Aer Lingus (from Dublin) Ⓦ www.aerlingus.com

British Airways Ⓦ www.ba.com

British Midland Ⓦ www.flybmi.com

Easyjet Ⓦ www.easyjet.com

Ryanair (to Malmö) Ⓦ www.ryanair.com

SAS (from UK and Dublin) Ⓦ www.scandinavian.net

Sterling Ⓦ www.sterlingticket.com

Varig Ⓦ www.varig.com

Many people are aware that air travel emits CO_2, which contributes to climate change. You may be interested in the possibility of lessening the environmental impact of your flight through Climate Care, which offsets your CO_2 by funding environmental projects around the world. Visit Ⓦ www.climatecare.org

By rail

This is normally the most expensive way to get to Copenhagen, unless you are visiting the city as part of an Interrail or Eurail trip. **Rail Europe** (Ⓦ www.raileurope.co.uk) can book the journey on-line.

A direct journey from the UK by rail will first involve a cross-Channel ferry or the **Eurostar** (Ⓣ 08705 186186 Ⓦ www.eurostar.com) to Brussels.

The monthly *Thomas Cook European Rail Timetable* has up-to-date schedules for international train services to Copenhagen and many Danish domestic routes. Ⓣ UK 01733 416477; USA 1 800 322 3834 Ⓦ www.thomascookpublishing.com

By water

If you plan to bring your own car to Copenhagen, you can take the ferry from Harwich, UK, to Esbjerg, Denmark with **DFDS Seaways** (Ⓣ UK 0871 522 9955; Denmark 33423000 Ⓦ www.dfds.co.uk). Departures are all year round, three times a week. From Esjberg, the trip by train is about five hours. If you are approaching Copenhagen via Oslo, the ferry takes around 16 hours.

ENTRY FORMALITIES

EU, US, Canadian, Australian and New Zealand citizens need only bring a valid passport. Other nationalities may need a visa.

For stays longer than three months a residence permit is required. EU citizens can apply for this while in Denmark, but other nationals must obtain one before arrival.

Immigration control is strict. Officers may ask for proof that you have a means of support for your stay in the country, that you have somewhere to stay and what the purpose of your visit is.

Residents of the UK, Ireland and other EU countries may bring into Denmark personal possessions and goods for personal use, including a reasonable amount of tobacco and alcohol, provided they have been bought in the EU.

Residents of non-EU countries, and EU residents arriving from a non-EU country, are limited to a maximum of: 400 cigarettes and 50 cigars or 50g (2 oz) tobacco; two litres (three bottles) of wine and one litre (approximately two pints) of spirits or liqueurs.

MONEY

Denmark is not part of the eurozone. Its currency, the krone (kr), is divided into 100 smaller units called øre. Notes come in 50, 100, 200, 500 and 1,000kr, and coins in 1, 2, 5, 10 and 20kr and 25 and 50 øre.

Banks are plentiful. Their opening hours are 10.00–16.00 weekdays, sometimes till 18.00 on Thursdays. There are 24-hour ATMs everywhere and they accept most internationally recognised debit and credit cards. Be careful at weekends as many of them run out of cash. Most banks will exchange a wide range of currencies and you can usually buy items on the plane or ferry in your own currency. Visa and Mastercard are widely accepted in shops and restaurants.

HEALTH, SAFETY & CRIME

No precautions in terms of vaccination or preventive medicines need be taken before visiting Copenhagen. Tap water is safe to drink. Healthcare is good.

EU citizens can use the Danish healthcare system although they must show the new European Health Insurance Card (EHIC) and may have to reclaim their expenses once they have returned home. A consultation with a doctor as a private patient will cost minimum 300kr.

Emergency treatment is free to all visitors and many countries outside the EU have similar reciprocal agreements. Travel insurance is still essential. Copenhagen is one of the safest cities in Europe, but as always, take care of belongings in crowded places such as the Central Station and Nørreport. Strøget in the early hours may be problematic, and in some areas around Vesterbro and Nørrebro you should be cautious. If you have anything stolen, report it immediately to the police and obtain a copy of their report for your insurance claim. A greater danger to visitors may be the system of cycle lanes, which run along most streets in the city, occasionally against the flow of traffic.

OPENING HOURS

On weekdays shops open at around 10.00 and close between 17.30 and 18.00, although some may stay open later. On Saturdays most shops are closed by mid-afternoon and will remain closed on Sundays, although bakeries open Sunday morning. Office hours are 09.00–16.00 Mon–Fri. Cafés and restaurants usually close around midnight on weekdays and 01.00–02.00 at the weekends, and clubs usually turn out around 05.00.

TOILETS

There are a few user-friendly public toilets in Copenhagen. The toilets in Central Station have good and inexpensive showers. Most public squares have pleasant public toilets, as do department stores.

CHILDREN

Copenhagen is an extremely child-friendly city. Most restaurants and café bars have child seats and highchairs and some even have child menus. Trains and buses have areas set aside for buggies and buses have easy access. Bike shops generally hire out children's bikes. The beaches and parks are great for children, especially in summer when there are often puppet shows.

Most museums and art galleries provide special children's sections. Out of town the Akvarium (see page 116) and the Experimentarium (see pages 117–20) have lots of hands-on exhibits, and Louisiana (see pages 121–2) has a children's art room where kids can experiment with different media. Bakken (see page 117) and Tivoli (see pages 82–3) are also likely to keep your kids entertained.

Nationalmuseet (see pages 84–5) has a children's museum and an early school room where they can explore the ink wells. Statens Museum for Kunst (see page 112) has a children's section where children can explore their artistic skills and there are also performances in the lobby.

Orlogsmuseet (see pages 99–100) has a children's section where they can handle guns and climb around a submarine. The Viking Ship Museum in Roskilde (see pages 128–9) has mocked-up ships and dressing up, as well as Viking board games and drawing activities. Tycho Brahe Planetarium (see page 83) is probably more suited to children than adults, particularly the IMAX shows.

▶ *Give the kids a breath of fresh air at the Frilandsmuseet*

You could also try the **Guinness World of Records Museum** (❸ Østergade 16) and **Ripley's Believe It or Not Museum** (❸ Rådhuspladsen), both run by Top Attractions Copenhagen (❶ 33323131 Ⓦ www.topattractions.dk). The open-air **Frilandsmuseet** ❸ Kongevejen 100, Lyngby ❶ 33134411 (Ⓦ www.natmus.dk ❶ 10.00–17.00 Tues–Sun ❷ Bus: 184; S-train: B, B+ to Sorgenfri) focuses on Danish rural life, and at weekends children can watch dancing demonstrations, take a ride in a horse and carriage and see costumed farm workers handling the animals.

COMMUNICATIONS
Internet
Internet cafés are a rarity in Copenhagen, since everyone is wired up at home. Most hotels offer free internet connections to their guests. Public libraries have computers with internet access. Try:

Det Kongelige Bibliotek ❸ Søren Kierkegaards Plads 1 ❶ 33474747 Ⓦ www.kb.dk ❶ 10.00–19.00 Mon–Fri, 10.00–14.00 Sat ❷ Bus: 66
Hovedbiblioteket ❸ Krystalgade 15 ❶ 33736060 Ⓦ www.bibliotek.kk.dk ❶ 10.00–19.00 Mon–Fri, 10.00–14.00 Sat
Københavns Universitetsbibliotek ❸ Fiolstræde 1 Ⓦ www.kb.dk ❶ 09.00–19.00 Mon–Thur, 09.00–18.00 Fri

Phone
Public telephones are either coin or card operated. The former take coins from 1kr to 20kr but do not give change. Cards can be bought at S-train stations and post offices. They come in denominations of 30, 50 and 100kr and work out slightly cheaper than using coins. A display in the phone box tells you how much credit you have left. Calls are cheaper after 19.30.

TELEPHONING DENMARK
The international dialling code for Denmark is 45. To dial any
of the Danish numbers in this book from your own country,
dial your own international access code (00 for the UK), then
45, then the eight-digit number. All private phones in Denmark
have eight digits and there are no area codes.

TELEPHONING ABROAD
To dial abroad from Denmark, dial 00 followed by your own
country's international code (UK 44, Ireland 353, USA and
Canada 1, Australia 61, New Zealand 64, South Africa 27)
and then the area code (leaving off the first 0) and number.

Directory enquiries is 118 and overseas directory enquiries
is 113 – be aware that the minute rate is astonishingly expensive
for these services. The Yellow Pages is on the internet
(ⓦ www.degulesider.dk).

Post
Letters weighing up to 50g to destinations within Denmark are
4.75kr. The same letter will cost 7.25kr to a European destination
and 8.25kr to the rest of the world.
Main Post Office ⓐ Tietgensgade 37 ① 33754475
ⓦ www.postdanmark.dk
Central Station Post Office ① 80207030 ⓛ 08.00–21.00 Mon–Fri,
10.00–16.00 Sat–Sun

ELECTRICITY

Denmark runs on 220V 50Hz AC. Danish sockets are round two-pin ones. Adapters are best bought in your home country, since Danish shops sell adapters for Danes going abroad rather than for visitors. Most hotels have square three-pin adapters you can borrow.

TRAVELLERS WITH DISABILITIES

Like most European cities Copenhagen builds new buildings and services with disabled people in mind. Buses have lowering ramps for wheelchairs and the newer hotels will have adapted rooms for disabled guests. Public toilets in newer buildings are disabled-friendly and the metro has lifts and easy access carriages. Older buildings are less accessible.

A free pamphlet is available from the tourist office which lists hotels, restaurants, museums and churches that are accessible to wheelchairs and have other facilities for disabled visitors.

For further information contact **Dansk Handicap Forbund** in Østerbro ⓐ Kollektivhuset, Hans Knudsens Plads 1a ❶ 39293555 Ⓦ www.dhf-net.dk ⓔ dhf-net.dk

TOURIST INFORMATION

Copenhagen Right Now The main tourist information centre in Copenhagen with a café, shop, free internet access and helpful staff who will book accommodation. Lots of free information and maps. ⓐ Vesterbrogade 4a ❶ 70222442 Ⓦ www.visitcopenhagen.dk ⓔ touristinfo@woco.dk 🕐 09.00–16.00 Mon–Fri, 09.00–14.00 Sat, Jan–Apr; 09.00–18.00 Mon–Sat, May & June; 09.00–20.00 Mon–Sat, 10.00–18.00 Sun, July & Aug; 09.00–16.00 Mon–Fri, 09.00–14.00 Sat, Sept–Apr

Helsingør tourist office Useful maps of the town and
accommodation information. ❸ Havnepladsen 3, Helsingør
❶ 49211333 Ⓦ www.visithelsingor.dk
Roskilde tourist office Maps, accommodation, free guide to
the town. ❸ Gullandstrasse 15, Roskilde ❶ 46316565
Ⓦ www.visitroskilde.com

BACKGROUND READING

Just As Well I'm Leaving by Michael Booth. Some humorous
comments on living among the Danes.
Miss Smilla's Feeling for Snow by Peter Høeg. Almost supernatural
crime thriller set in Christianshavn.
The Complete Fairy Tale by Hans Christian Andersen. Get in the
mood for the city with some very weird fairytales.
Copenhagen by Michael Frayn. Strange play which discusses
quantum physics, loyalty and betrayal.
Seven Gothic Tales by Karen Blixen. The Danish writer's take
on the gothic.
The Buildings of Europe: Copenhagen by Christopher Woodward.
Illustrated guide to many of Copenhagen's architecturally
interesting buildings.
A Short History of Denmark by Stig Hornshøj-Møller. Good, brief
account of several thousand years of history.

Emergencies

Emergency number for police, ambulance or fire service ☎ 112

MEDICAL SERVICES
Doctor
Your hotel will have a list of local doctors, otherwise go to the hospital. Fees are around 300kr plus and must be paid in cash. Keep receipts if you want to make an insurance claim.
Emergency doctor on call overnight ☎ 70130041 🕐 16.00–08.00

Dentist
The tourist office can recommend a dentist. Dentists' fees are paid in cash.
Emergency dental service ⓐ Oslo Plads 14 ☎ 35380251 🕐 20.00–21.30 Mon–Fri, 10.00–12.00 & 20.00–21.00 Sat & Sun

Hospitals
Skadestuen (Accident and Emergency departments) can be found at:
Amager Hospital ⓐ Italiensvej 1, Amager ☎ 32343234
Bispebjerg Hospital ⓐ Bispebjerg Bakke 23 ☎ 35313135
Frederiksberg Hospital ⓐ Nordre Fasanvej 57, Frederiksberg ☎ 38163522

Pharmacies
Most pharmacies (*Apotek*) keep general shopping hours. You can recognise them from the sign *Apotek* above the door.
24-hour pharmacy at Steno Apotek, opposite Central Station
ⓐ Vesterbogade 6 ☎ 33148266

POLICE
Near Central Station ⓐ Halmtorvet 20 ⓣ 33251448
Near Kongens Nytorv ⓐ Store Kongensgade 100 ⓣ 33931448

Lost property
For missing credit cards call:
Amex ⓣ 80010021
Diners Club ⓣ 36737373
Mastercard & Eurocard ⓣ 80016098
Visa ⓣ 80018588
Be aware that the 8001 numbers are toll-free but cannot be called using mobile phones.

For lost property on trains contact:
Central Station ⓐ Reventlowsgade 9 ⓣ 33545681

EMERGENCY PHRASES

Help!
Hjælp!
Yehlb!

Can you help me?
Kan du hjæpe mig?
Ka do yehlbeh mai?

Call an ambulance/a doctor/the police!
Ring efter en ambulance/en læge/politiet!
Ring ehfda in ahmboolahnseh/in leh-eh/porlitee-eht!

Lost Property on buses is a little complicated as there are different operators and offices for the different routes. Here are some of the main routes:

1A ❶ 36789004
2A ❶ 72302668
5A ❶ 72302700
6A ❶ 20909621
250S ❶ 32961916
350S ❶ 72302759

EMBASSIES & CONSULATES

In the event of theft or injury your country's embassy will expect you to go through the emergency channels in Copenhagen. They will also expect you to have taken out travel insurance which will cover your needs. If the emergency is of your own making, such as an arrest for drunk driving or disorderly conduct, the embassy will be unable to intervene. Embassies can, however, issue a replacement passport.

Australian ⓐ Dampfærgevej 26 ❶ 70263676
Ⓦ www.denmark.embassy.gov.au
British ⓐ Kastelsvej 36–40 ❶ 77348651 Ⓦ www.britishembassy.dk
Canadian ⓐ Kristen Bernikowsgade 1 ❶ 33483200 Ⓦ www.canada.dk
Irish ⓐ Østbanegade 21 ❶ 35423233
US ⓐ Dag Hammarskjölds Allé 24 ❶ 35417100 Ⓦ www.usembassy.dk

❿ *Copenhagen is safe and easy to get around*

WHAT'S IN YOUR GUIDEBOOK?

Independent authors Impartial up-to-date information from our travel experts who meticulously source local knowledge.

Experience Thomas Cook's 165 years in the travel industry and guidebook publishing enriches every word with expertise you can trust.

Travel know-how Contributions by thousands of staff around the globe, each one living and breathing travel.

Editors Travel-publishing professionals, pulling everything together to craft a perfect blend of words, pictures, maps and design.

You, the traveller We deliver a practical, no-nonsense approach to information, geared to how you really use it.

SPOT A CITY IN SECONDS

This great range of pocket city guides will have you in the know in no time. Lightweight and packed with detail on the most important things from shopping and sights to non-stop nightlife, they knock spots off chunkier, clunkier versions. Titles include:

Amsterdam	Bratislava	Glasgow	Madrid	Salzburg
Antwerp	Bruges	Gothenburg	Marrakech	Sarajevo
Athens	Brussels	Granada	Milan	Seville
Barcelona	Bucharest	Hamburg	Monte Carlo	Sofia
Belfast	Budapest	Hanover	Munich	Stockholm
Belgrade	Cardiff	Helsinki	Naples	Strasbourg
Berlin	Cologne	Hong Kong	New York	St Petersburg
Bilbao	Copenhagen	Istanbul	Nice	Tallinn
Bologna	Cork	Kiev	Oslo	Toulouse
	Dubai	Krakow	Palermo	Turin
	Dublin	Leipzig	Palma	Valencia
	Dubrovnik	Lille	Paris	Venice
	Düsseldorf	Lisbon	Prague	Verona
	Edinburgh	Ljubljana	Porto	Vienna
	Florence	London	Reykjavik	Vilnius
	Frankfurt	Lyon	Riga	Warsaw
	Gdansk		Rome	Zagreb
	Geneva			Zurich
	Genoa			

CITY SPOTS
HAMBURG

CITY SPOTS
VILNIUS

BILBAO

CITY SPOTS
NEW YORK

CITY SPOTS
GLASGOW

ACKNOWLEDGEMENTS & FEEDBACK

Editorial/project management: Lisa Plumridge
Copy editor: Monica Guy
Layout: Pat Hinsley
Proofreader: Wendy Janes

The publishers would like to thank the following individuals and
organisations for supplying their copyright photographs for this book:
Adrian Beesley/istockphoto.com, page 71; Nicol Foulkes, pages 7, 9, 17,
24, 30, 65, 69, 73, 75, 79 & 92; Tristan de Haas/istockphoto.com, page 59;
Hotel Alexandra, page 36; Hans Laubel/istockphoto.com, page 107;
Pat Levy, pages 15, 19, 45, 47, 54, 94, 102, 120, 122, 141 & 155; Radisson SAS
Royal Hotel, page 39; Kamil Sobócki/Dreamstime.com, pages 5 & 20;
Kenny Viese/istockphoto.com, page 40; Visit Copenhagen, pages 115
& 147; Visit Denmark, pages 1, 13, 21, 62, 81, 111, 127, 128, 136 & 139.

Send your thoughts to
books@thomascook.com

- Found a great bar, club, shop or must-see sight that we don't feature?
- Like to tip us off about any information that needs a little updating?
- Want to tell us what you love about this handy little guidebook and
  more importantly how we can make it even handier?

Then here's your chance to tell all! Send us ideas, discoveries and
recommendations today and then look out for your valuable input
in the next edition of this title.

Email the above address (stating the title) or write to:
CitySpots Project Editor, Thomas Cook Publishing, PO Box 227,
Coningsby Road, Peterborough PE3 8SB, UK.